For my Dad,

Enjoy, it's really interesting!

all my love

your

Clare
xxx

The Japanese Occupation
1 9 4 2 — 1 9 4 5

NATIONAL HERITAGE BOARD
National Archives of Singapore

The Japanese Occupation
1942 – 1945

A Pictorial Record of Singapore During the War

TIMES EDITIONS

Text:	Tan Beng Luan
	Irene Quah
Translation:	Tan Beng Luan
	Chung Lai Beng
	Wong Kum Oi
Photography:	James Toh
Editing:	Jonathan Griffiths
	Shova Loh
Design:	Tuck Loong

© 1996 National Archives of Singapore
Reprinted 1998, 2001

Published by Times Editions
An imprint of Times Media Pte Ltd
A member of the Times Publishing Group
Times Centre, 1 New Industrial Road
Singapore 536196
Fax: (65) 2854871 Tel: (65) 2848844
E-mail: te@tpl.com.sg
Online Book Store: http://www.timesone.com.sg/te

Times Subang
Lot 46, Subang Hi-Tech Industrial Park
Batu Tiga, 40000 Shah Alam
Selangor Darul Ehsan, Malaysia
Fax & Tel: (603) 7363517
E-mail: cchong@tpg.com.my

Printed in Malaysia

ISBN 981 204 741 7 (English edition)
ISBN 981 204 742 5 (Chinese edition)

MAKE FORTUNE
BY COOPERATING
WITH JAPAN

p. 1:   Japanese tanks enter the city of Singapore.
p. 2:   "Yes or no?" Lieutenant General Yamashita presses for British surrender.
p. 4 top: Anti-British leaflet promoting business with the Japanese.
p. 4 bottom: Donation certificate for the China relief fund effort.
pp. 6–7:   Sinking of HMS *Prince of Wales* and HMS *Repulse*.
p. 8:   Japanese Occupation propaganda publications.

National Library Board (Singapore)
Cataloguing in Publication Data

The Japanese occupation 1942-1945 :
a pictorial record of Singapore during
the war / [text by Tan Beng Luan,
Irene Quah]. — Singapore : Times
Editions, 1996
p.   cm.

At head of title: National Heritage
Board, National Archives of
Singapore.

Includes bibliography and index
ISBN: 981-204-741-7

1. World War, 1939-1945—
Campaigns—Singapore—Pictorial
works.

2. Singapore—History—Japanese
Occupation, 1942-1945.
I. Tan, Beng Luan.
II. Quah, Irene.
III. Singapore. National Heritage
Board.
IV. National Archives of Singapore.

DS610.55
940. 5425— dc21
959.5703 – dc21
SLS96111646

To those who were killed in the Japanese invasion and occupation of Singapore, and for those who love peace.

THE WORLD

1931		Japan invades Manchuria.
1937	July	Japan's total invasion of China.
1939	September	Germany invades Poland.
		Britain and France declare war on Germany.
1940	April	Germany invades Denmark and Norway.
1940	May	Holland and Belgium surrender.
1940	June	France falls to Germany.
1940	August	Germany bombs Britain.
1941	June	Germany invades Russia.
1941	July	Japan occupies Indo-China.
1941	December	Japan attacks Pearl Harbor.
1942	January	Japan occupies Malaya.
1942	March	Japan enters Burma and Indonesia.
1942	May	Japan occupies the Philippines.
1942	June	Japan loses sea battle at Midway.
1943	July	Italy makes peace with the Allies.
1944	March	The Japanese mount offensive in Burma.
1944	August	France is liberated.
1944	September	Allied troops enter Germany.
1945	May	British troops reoccupy Burma.
		Germany's formal surrender.
1945	August	Atomic bomb drops on Hiroshima and Nagasaki.
1945	September	The Japanese and Allied leaders sign surrender document aboard the battleship USS *Missouri*.

SINGAPORE

1931		The Chinese form the Shantung Relief Fund Committee.
1937	August	The Chinese set up the Singapore China Relief Fund Committee, led by Tan Kah Kee.
1938		Naval base at Sembawang completed.
1940		Local coastal defence begins.
1941		Arrival of reinforcements. Recruitment of local volunteers in various service units.
1941	December	Singapore Volunteer Corps mobilised. Japan drops bombs on Singapore.
1942	February	Lieutenant General A.E. Percival surrenders to the Japanese; surrender document signed at Ford factory. Japanese Occupation begins. Purge of the Chinese begins.
1942	March	Rationing system begins. Formation of Overseas Chinese Association.
1942	April	Registration of families. Schools reopened teaching Japanese language.
1942	September	Auxiliary Police System introduced.
1943	May	Recruitment of *Heiho* (auxiliary servicemen).
1943	August	Mass evacuation to Endau and Bahau.
1943	December	Labour Service Corps introduced.
1945	May	Bombing by B-29s.
1945	September	Formal surrender of the Japanese at Municipal Building.

南光週刊

第五十五期

卷首...

太陽 TAIJO TAIYO ダイヤウ

SUEKIKO TODOROKI
YUKIKO TODOROKI
女明星 轟夕起子
トドロキ ユキコ

聖戰畫帖

戰ふ東條首相

小田俊與編・著

Contents

Foreword

The Japanese Occupation of Singapore lasted for a short period from February 1942 to September 1945 but its scars remain deeply etched in the minds of those who lived through it. Over 54 years have lapsed since the fall of Singapore, yet many older Singaporeans will remember vividly the brutalities meted out by Japanese soldiers. The massacre of thousands of Chinese, and the defilement and carnage of defenceless ordinary people were some of the gruesome aspects that were identified with this brief but turbulent period.

Younger generations of Singaporeans who have grown up in a safe and secure environment over the past 30 years will find it difficult to comprehend or have a feel for the hardships of war. Nor will they really understand the meaning of deprivation, food shortages, and a total loss of freedom. This publication tries to bridge this experience gap.

The Japanese Military Administration left no written records behind in Singapore. To address the unavailability of official historical data, the National Archives of Singapore acquired photographs, artifacts and paraphernalia from private individuals and institutions. In addition to this, in 1981, the Oral History Department (now Oral History Centre) undertook to record the reminiscences of local people who had experienced the war and the Occupation. Up to now, we have interviewed some 175 persons. Currently, we are trying to fill the gaps by interviewing wartime Japanese military officials and civil administrators who were stationed in Singapore from 1942 to 1945. Quite a number of the oral history interview extracts have been used in this new publication to describe intimately what life was like during the Occupation.

There is no doubt that older readers will feel a sense of familiarity with the scenes depicted in the photographs, or events described by the documents. But for many Singaporeans who were too young then to be associated with the events of 1942 to 1945, it will be a fresh insight to understanding the extreme hardships suffered by most Singaporeans and the tribulations we had undergone as an occupied country.

This publication is an expanded edition of *The Japanese Occupation: Singapore 1942–1945* which was first printed in 1985. It has both English and Chinese editions. I hope this publication will be as well received as the previous editions which had seven print runs within a span of ten years.

LIM CHEE ONN
CHAIRMAN
NATIONAL HERITAGE BOARD

Tan Kah Kee (left),
chairman of the Singapore
China Relief Fund
Committee (SCRFC).

Pre-war Singapore

Japan had risen to her prominent military strength by 1919, shortly after the First World War. Asia was a source of raw materials vital to the Japanese economy and an almost limitless market for the products of Japanese industry. Japan was prepared, at all cost, to secure her status as a great power and, more ambitiously, as the master of Asia.

In Singapore, many Chinese considered China their motherland – identification with Singapore as a homeland was politically inconceivable at that time. Thus, in 1937, when China declared war on Japan after their troops clashed at Marco Polo Bridge near Beijing on July 7, Chinese workers and students, led by Singapore communist activists, reacted promptly by organising relief fund activities in aid of China's war effort.

Japan's aggressive move threatened the European colonial presence in Asia. To contain the communist influence, the British Colonial Government chose Tan Kah Kee to coordinate the Chinese relief fund activities. The Chinese community leaders eventually took centre stage and the Singapore China Relief Fund Committee (SCRFC) was founded.

Singapore soon became the centre of an anti-Japanese mass movement which involved Chinese from all walks of life, including the Straits-born Chinese and other Chinese in Southeast Asia. Fund-raising branches were set up in urban and rural areas. Funds were raised through monthly and special donations by

Above: The Sino-Japanese War broke out on July 7, 1937. This sparked off widespread anti-Japanese sentiment among the overseas Chinese. A 6-year-old Singapore boy's drawing shows a Chinese man being killed by a Japanese sword.

Left: The Singapore Chinese quickly rallied to help their compatriots in China. On August 15, 1937, Tan Kah Kee, an entrepreneur highly respected by the Chinese community, was elected to lead the Singapore China Relief Fund Committee (SCRFC).

Right: The headquarters of the SCRFC was located at the Ee Hoe Hean Club at 43 Bukit Pasoh Road. Its aim was to coordinate the relief efforts of all Chinese dialect groups in Singapore.

employees and businesses, festival donations by members of the public, the sale of flags and paper flowers and organised events such as concerts, games and variety shows. According to the figures provided by Tan Kah Kee, the amount sent to China by the Chinese in Southeast Asia from 1937 to 1942 was $5,530 million (pre-war China currency).

To disrupt the Japanese economy, some Chinese, indirectly assisted and protected by certain Chinese community leaders in the SCRFC, organised unlawful groups to punish Chinese merchants trading in Japanese goods. The most notable group was the Chinese National Emancipation Vanguard Corps. The measures taken included sending threatening letters to the merchants and splashing tar on their signboards. These unlawful groups also placed the Japanese community and agents of the Japanese Government in Singapore under surveillance.

The Chinese involvement in the anti-Japanese movement was in turn closely watched by Japanese agents. The information they sent back was later used by Japanese decision makers in Tokyo to firm up their Chinese policy for the occupied territories. ∎

Below: Fund-raising branches of the SCRFC were set up in both rural and urban areas, as well as by occupational groups. Members were given badges such as this for identification.

Hau Say Huan (left) with Tan Kah Kee.

THE POWER OF PATRIOTISM

"After the founding of the SCRFC, its branches were everywhere – in shops, factories, warehouses. Every worker volunteered to donate 10% or 5% of his income. In schools, pocket money given to the students by their parents, we gave every school a relief fund box, students would drop money into the box. We organised some teams, each took care of certain numbers of schools and clearing the boxes once a week.

"Factories would list down names of workers and their monthly donations. We also organised 'popular speeches'. Hau Say Huan, Lau Boh Tan, Chew Hean Swee and I gave speeches in three or four places each night. Wherever we went, we organised a relief fund branch. We taught the villagers how to organise things.

"There were also patriotic groups [not affiliated to SCRFC]. They were in every street and almost every shop had one such group member to collect information. No one paid them. They did it for the survival of the nation [China] and people, they didn't want to be the slaves of the imperialists. Whoever bought Japanese goods would soon be found out by the patriotic groups. They also helped in propaganda work. Every factory, every worker helped in the mobilisation and made it [the relief fund efforts] prevalent. That zest of patriotism touched us deeply."

—*Ng Aik Huan, key member, SCRFC*

Far left: Lau Boh Tan

*Left: Ng Aik Huan
with Tan Kah Kee*

Right: A group of youths from the Queen Street area helped raise funds by selling home-made paper flowers.

Below: Women entertainers organised their own teams, selling flowers to raise funds.

Left and above: In December 1938, the Wuhan Choir from China toured Singapore and Malaya for 17 months to raise funds. Their patriotic songs had a great impact on the local Chinese. An album was cut to commemorate their visit.

Right: Artist Xu Beihong painted the famous "Put Down Your Whip", circa 1939. It shows a sketch being performed in the street to build up patriotic feelings in one of the Japanese-occupied territories in China.

Below: "Selling Flowers" – lyrics by Pan Kuo Chu (Pan Shou, now a Singapore national artist) and music by Xia Zhi Qiu (choirmaster of Wuhan Choir) – became a very popular song to boost the morale of the fund-raisers.

卖花詞　潘国渠詞

先生！買一朶花吧！　先生！買一朶花吧！

　这是自由之花呀，这是解放之花呀，
　買了花、　　救了国家。

先生！買一朶花吧！　先生！買一朶花吧！

　不是要你的愛花，不是要你的賞花，
　買了花，　　救了自家。

先生！買一朶花吧！　先生！買一朶花吧！

Left: The fund-raising branch of the Hawkers' Association raised $937 and a receipt dated October 14, 1940, was issued.

Below: A certificate of appreciation dated October 13, 1940, was awarded to an individual who made a substantial donation to the relief fund.

DEVOTION OF SCRFC LEADERS

"Our expenses, salaries and odds and ends were all donated by members of the SCRFC. Funds raised were never touched, all put into the bank [to be remitted to China]. Tan Kah Kee had to attend to many things. He worked here [Ee Hoe Hean Club] for about 16 hours a day. He had to meet people, hold confidential meetings, make decisions, meet reporters and read many letters. The secretary would have to show him these letters, he would then give instructions. He stayed in the Ee Hoe Hean Club and hadn't been home for many years. His children even had to come here to pay their New Year respects. He was so busy here that he had no time to attend to his family matters.

"Ng Aik Huan and Lau Boh Tan came here every day. Ng Aik Huan gave speeches at selling flowers occasions and mass rallies. He was very articulate and could draw audiences. Lau Boh Tan was very strong in organisational skills and he wrote well. Both were the right-hand men of Tan Kah Kee."

—Lim Hoon, secretary, SCRFC Secretariat

Below: An anti-Japanese boycott organised by some radical groups pressed the local Chinese to stop buying, selling or using Japanese goods. A death threat was sent by a "Singapore Assassin Corps" to a merchant allegedly involved in such activities.

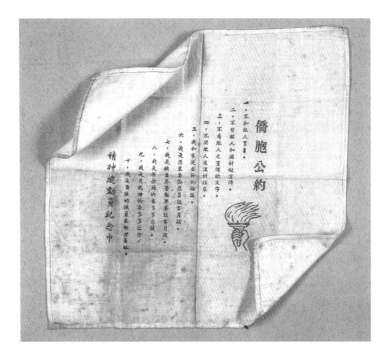

Above: A "Compatriot Pledge" handkerchief was given to each participant attending the gathering "Mobilising Our Spirits." The pledge reads:

> Not to trade with the enemy.
> Not to propagate for the enemy and traitors.
> Not to read the enemy's propaganda materials.
> Not to communicate with the enemy and traitors.
> For the relief work, my family and I shall be thrifty.
> As an employer, I shall encourage my staff to make monthly contributions.
> As an employee, I shall pledge a monthly contribution.
> I am rich, I shall give as much as I should.
> I am strong, I shall give as much assistance as I should.
> I am a Relief Fund employee, I shall do my best.

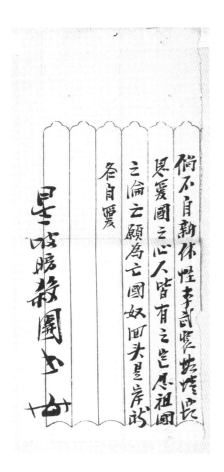

Above: To strengthen the solidarity of overseas Chinese in the relief fund effort, over 180 Chinese representatives from the Philippines, Indonesia, Indo-China and Malaya gathered at the Chinese High School in Bukit Timah Road on October 10, 1938, to form the Southseas China Relief Fund Federation (SCRFF). Its headquarters was also located at the Ee Hoe Hean Club.

Above left: The SCRFF was chaired by (from left) Tjhung Sie Gan of Indonesia, Chin Chan Boey of Malaya, Tan Kah Kee of Singapore, Ong Chuan Seng of the Philippines and Tan Sau Chi of Vietnam.

Above right: Key secretariat members of the SCRFF were (from right) Pan Kuo Chu (Pan Shou) and Lee Tiat Ming.

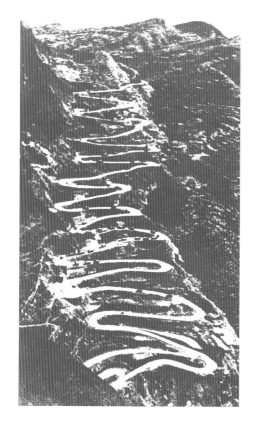

Below: In response to China's request, the SCRFF recruited some 3,200 volunteer drivers and mechanics from Southeast Asia. Badges such as this were given to volunteers.

Left: A Yunnan-Burma highway through the mountains was used to transport supplies to Chungking, wartime capital of China. The Chinese Government requested volunteer drivers and mechanics to work on the road.

Above: Volunteer drivers and mechanics, besides risking their lives driving under constant Japanese air raids, also faced shortages of food and clothing.

Right: This poster shows that the British also appealed to the Chinese for support after Germany's bombing of London in August 1940.

Right: The Japanese military presence in Indo-China in September 1940 put the British on guard. With a military strategy focused on sea defence, fortresses and pillboxes were built to defend the southern coast of Singapore.

Left and below: Soldiers of the Manchester Regiment built up the beach defence with wire entanglements, minefields and log barriers to make amphibious operations difficult.

Left: Local people were recruited to help in the civil defence work. An Air Raid Precaution (ARP) member was given a card which indicated the district he was responsible for.

AIR RAID PRECAUTION

"I joined the ARP as an ordinary member. We had about 30 members in our team and were stationed at Sutton Close. As an ARP, my main responsibility was to go round my area at night and see that no lights in our area were visible from outside or from the sky. We were also required to report casualties, if any, after each air raid. We were not given uniforms but a helmet with an ARP mark on it. We were in charge of the Tanglin area."

—Ismail Zain, ARP member

Above: Badge of the ARP.

Left: Members of the ARP carried out regular weekly mass demonstrations to keep the residents bomb-alert and informed.

Right: ARP members were also trained to operate sirens during air raids and to help residents to air raid shelters.

Right: Those enrolled in the Medical Auxiliary Service (MAS) were also given identification cards.

Left: The Singapore Volunteer Corps (SVC) was established in 1854. It consisted of the European, Eurasian, Chinese and Malay Companies.

Left and far left: A recruitment drive for more SVC members took place in October 1941.

Above (top): Recruits were also enlisted for the Royal Army Medical Corps, Royal Army Service Corps and the Malay Regiment.

Above (bottom): The Malay Regiment was a regular force formed in 1933 in Malaya. After the outbreak of war in Europe, Singapore took in new recruits who were joined by the Regiment's members from Malaya and stationed at Pasir Panjang.

By 1941 Japanese acts of aggression in Asia became more intensified. A considerable number of reinforcements arrived in Singapore in 1941 to join the Malaya Command.
Right and below: Australian soldiers and nurses.
Left: Royal Corps of Signals, Royal Artillery and Naval Engineers.
Bottom: Indian troops from British-ruled India.

Far left: Manoeuvres were carried out to demonstrate British readiness to face the impending Japanese attack.

Left and below: The Manchester Regiment and Gurkhas trained in the jungle.

Right: Bren carriers and their crews during a military exercise in October 1941.

Left: Northover projector, an anti-tank measure of the battalion of the Gordon Highlanders.

Above: Requests for air defence reinforcements were ignored by the British Command. There were 158 operational aircraft on the eve of the Japanese attack.

Left: HMS Durham of the Eastern Fleet on exercise in the Singapore Straits in November 1941. The British prime minister, Winston Churchill, believed the most important defence of Singapore was the Eastern Fleet.

Right: To counter Japanese espionage work in Singapore, the Argyle and Sutherland Highlanders carried out an anti-Fifth Column exercise in 1941. These officers underwent a training exercise that included role-playing. This photograph shows two trainees, one disguised as a priest, the other playing the part of a local informer.

THE FIFTH COLUMN

"Japanese residents here each had his background as well as activities circle. Their aims were to disturb the economy and the law and order here. They had men in every corner. The most famous one was a shop at Beach Road, Sin Tai Chong. It sold spare parts for fishing boats. Later, [we] knew it was an intelligence agency of the Japanese Navy. Those who worked in the shop were Taiwanese.

"After the Japanese invasion [of Malaya], those who worked there all became Japanese interpreters. There were Japanese residents at Old Race Course Road, Serangoon Road and Jalan Besar. I lived there as well, so that I could gather some information about them. They were all bachelors and rented houses from the Indians and the Malays. They all had assignments and were what we called the Fifth Column.

"When Singapore was bombed, those suspected by me had disappeared. The Chinese National Emancipation Vanguard Corps had friends in the British [Colonial] Government, so we kept them informed, gave them information. However, they wouldn't simply take our word, they would investigate and confirm the facts before taking any action."

—*See Hong Peng, leader, Chinese National Emancipation Vanguard Corps*

Above: Suspected Japanese spies were arrested and sent to prisons in British-ruled India. In November 1941, about 450 Japanese who resided in Singapore left. Their luggage was carefully searched for intelligence materials.

Japanese victory.

Fall of Singapore

Singapore, a crown colony of the King of England, had long been identified as a unique strategic point to defend the interests of the British Empire if she were to be involved in a naval war in the Pacific. With this in mind, a modernised naval base at Sembawang was completed in 1938. Throughout the 1930s, the British continued to base their military strategy on sea defence, expecting the enemy to come from the South China Sea. Consequently, little was done to develop the beach defence on the northern shore of Singapore.

Above: Japanese soldiers crossing the causeway linking Singapore to Johore in Malaya.

Manoeuvres were carried out to demonstrate the British readiness to withstand the impending Japanese aggression. But the defence plan was executed halfheartedly, as Britain was more concerned with her engagement in the European war than channelling essential military resources, especially the air force, to the Far East. It was not until the Japanese made a sudden landing on Malaya's east coast that more British troops were hastily sent in from India, Australia and England. Yet, many of them were neither trained nor equipped for jungle warfare.

The Japanese, on the other hand, had worked out their attack strategy carefully by using intelligence collected directly or indirectly from the Japanese community in Malaya and Singapore. There were approximately 80,000 British combat men compared to 35,000 Japanese combat men. However, the Japanese overpowered the British in the air, as they had 459 army planes and 158 naval planes. The British Navy and Army did not have substantial or adequate air cover, and this factor greatly influenced the outcome of the war in Malaya and Singapore.

The arrival of the British Eastern Fleet, including HMS Repulse *and the new battleship, HMS* Prince of Wales *(above), on December 2, 1941, strengthened the public's confidence in the British defence capability.*

To secure political support from the locals, the British drew on the support of the Chinese community leaders and the communists, forming them into one action group, known as the Singapore Chinese Mobilisation Council, on December 30, 1941. However, it could not withhold the rapid British retreat or the Japanese advance down the Malayan Peninsula.

It took the Japanese only 55 days to occupy Malaya. On February 15, 1942, owing to losses suffered by the British from enemy action, water, petrol, food and ammunition were practically exhausted. The British found themselves unable to continue the fight any longer, and they capitulated to the Japanese after seven days of Singapore defence. The British official history states that during the defence of Malaya and Singapore, the total battle casualties of the British, Australian, Indian and volunteer local forces were about 8,700.

The fall of Singapore, the impregnable fortress of the British Empire in the East, marks the beginning of a brief but tumultuous chapter of Singapore history.■

Right: At 7:55 a.m. (Hawaiian time) on December 7, 1941, the Japanese launched a surprise attack on the US Fleet at Pearl Harbor in Hawaii. The United States entered the war.

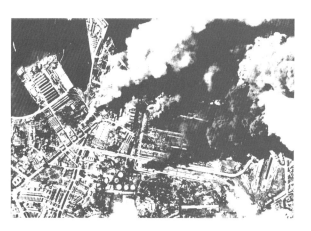

Above: In the very early hours of December 8, 1941, Japanese troops landed at Kota Bharu, capital of Kelantan, Malaya. All British forces, including the volunteer forces of Malaya and Singapore, were mobilised for the defence of Malaya.

Top: At around 4 a.m. on December 8, 1941, Japanese aircraft bombed Singapore.
Bottom: On December 10, 1941, HMS Repulse *and HMS* Prince of Wales
encountered Japanese bombers off the Kuantan coast and were sunk.

Admiral Sir Tom Phillips (right), commander of the Eastern Fleet, went down with HMS Prince of Wales. The loss of the two battleships severely shook public confidence in Britain's ability to defend Singapore.

CAUGHT UNPREPARED

"My company was mobilised on the 1st of December 1941. It had been decided by the higher-ups that we would serve in Singapore. The whole battalion came down on the 4th of December and was stationed at St. Patrick's School.

"It was clear to me that there was such unpreparedness on this island. We were doing things like putting down the wire on the beaches from St. Patrick's drain, right up to the Chinese Swimming Club, putting up tents for other units and digging trenches. We were told that our role would be counter-attacks on the beaches. We had to study all the pillboxes from St. Patrick's drain, right up to Jurong River. That is a very long distance.

"On the 11th of February 1942 we were told to cover the withdrawal of British troops from Changi … [Then] I got an order to take up a defensive position along Farrer Road/Adam Road. So instead of going to Changi, we had to go the other way. When we arrived somewhere in the vicinity of the 6th Avenue, Bukit Timah Road, I sent a note to the battalion headquarters that we were in position. But to my amazement, I had an order to withdraw! And this seemed to be the pattern. For no rhyme or reason, withdraw, withdraw, withdraw."

—Herman Marie de Souza, commander, Eurasian Company, Malacca Volunteer Force

THE BRITISH MALAYAN COMMAND

Air Chief Marshal Sir Robert Brooke-Popham,
Commander-in-Chief, Far East.

Lieutenant General A.E. Percival,
General Officer Commanding Malaya.

Major General Gordon Bennett,
Commander of the Australian Force.

Lieutenant General Sir Lewis Heath,
Commander of the Indian Division.

THE JAPANESE COMMAND

Field Marshal Count Hisaichi Terauchi, Supreme Commander of Southern Force.

Lieutenant General Tomoyuki Yamashita, Commander, 25th Army.

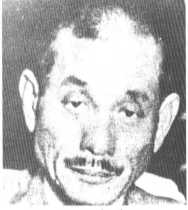

Lieutenant General Takuro Matsui, Commander of the 5th Division.

Lieutenant General Renya Mutaguchi, Commander of the 18th Division.

Lieutenant General Takuma Nishimura, Commander of the Imperial Guards Division.

*Above and right:
Swiftly and steadily,
Japanese troops pushed
southwards.*

*Left and right:
British troops
were forced to
take up
defensive
positions as
each major
Malayan town
fell to the
Japanese.*

Left: In Singapore, on December 30, 1941, Governor Sir Shenton Thomas invited Tan Kah Kee to form the Singapore Chinese Mobilisation Council to assist the British. Its headquarters was in the Chin Kang Hui Kuan (Chin Kang Clan Association) building at Bukit Pasoh Road.

Right (top and bottom): The Council set up the Defence Corps and Labour Corps to help maintain law and order, supply labourers for the armed forces and help the needy.

DALFORCE

"I did not have any other ability but this [fighting the Japanese]. I didn't think I would be safe behind the line. Since it wasn't safe, I might as well go to the front to resist them, to fight them. If I could kill one Japanese, my sacrifice would be rewarded. If I could kill one more, it would be a bonus. So I was pleased to go and register.

"We gathered in Nan Chiao School [Kim Yam Road] for training. I believe it was less than two weeks. We learnt marching and shooting. We had no uniforms – only an armband. I learnt about shooting in China, therefore I was given a rifle and three bullets. The rest of the people were given some sort of bird rifles. When we saw it, we were very disappointed. Gave us such stuff, what's the use? How could we fight the enemy with such arms? By then, the Japanese were already in Johore."

—*Teo Choon Hong, Dalforce*

Left: The British also allowed the Malayan Communist Party (MCP) to help set up a Singapore Overseas Chinese Anti-Japanese Volunteer Army, also known as Dalforce. It was led by a British officer, J.D. Dalley. Recruits were given minimal military training and armaments were inadequate. This letter, dated January 25, 1942, bears the Dalforce seal.

Above (top and bottom): As the situation deteriorated, many British and local civilians were evacuated from Singapore. Those who could not get away sought refuge wherever they could.

BATTLE FOR SINGAPORE (FEBRUARY 1942)

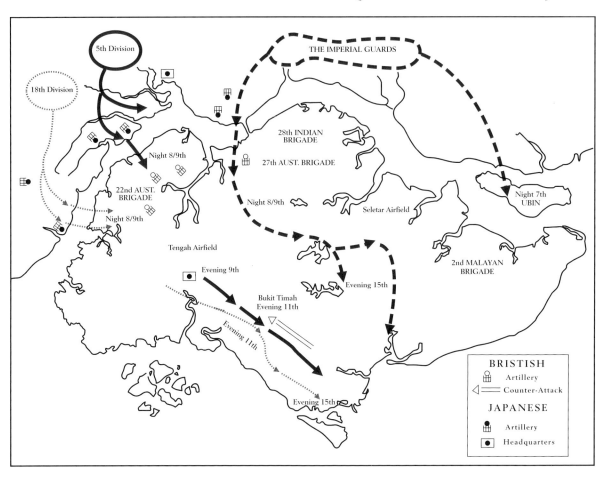

Above: On January 31, the Japanese entered and occupied Johore Bahru.
On February 7, the Imperial Guards or the Konoe Division occupied Pulau Ubin.
On February 9, the Japanese 5th and 18th Divisions made an amphibious landing on the northwest coast of Singapore.
After this, they swept inland, forcing the British troops to give up their positions at Choa Chu Kang Village, Ama Keng Village and Tengah Airfield.

Right: On January 31, 1942, the Japanese Army occupied Johore Bahru. All British forces retreated to Singapore and the causeway was blown up. Yamashita repositioned his forces for the attack on Singapore.

CASUALTIES

"I think it was the 8th of February, they [the Japanese] began the most intensive bombardment during the night, using everything. The whole of that northern coast was pounded. To give some idea how effective and terrific it was, 60 Gurkhas that night were killed or injured, just in the 2/2 Gurkha Regiment.

"In the end, we were given orders to fall back. And I came back into the town, and here, it was possible to see for the first time the extent of civilian casualties. I recall one of our junior officers, he had the body of a Tamil girl lying across his knees, weeping over the body. The girl had been killed by the blast. I myself carried a boy, he had been peppered with stones that had been thrown out by a bomb. This poor little Chinese boy, hair cut in a circular fringe, didn't cry, he was just simply shivering. I gently carried him down to the road and got an ambulance to take him. I just hoped that somebody would be able to take the stones out and cauterise the wounds. I can still see his face."

—*Stanley Warren, Artillery 344 Battery, 135th Regiment*

Left: The Japanese began their siege of Singapore with constant aerial bombardment and shelling, causing high civilian casualties.

Left: In the early hours of February 9, 1942, covered by their heavy artillery, the Japanese 5th and 18th Divisions made an amphibious landing on the northwest coast of Singapore.

Above: Dalforce members, together with the 22nd Australian Brigade, were there to face wave upon wave of Japanese attacks. They resisted stubbornly all night and the Japanese suffered heavy casualties. This photograph of Dalforce members in training is taken from film footage.

JAPANESE LANDING

"Shortly after the landing of the first batch, they suffered 42 casualties in one hour. I was in the second batch. We were about 54 altogether. When we reached the middle of the Straits, we encountered heavy firing from machine guns. Luckily, they were aimed at about fifty metres away from us. At that time, we wondered what the first batch was doing, as they should have been covering us. Why did the enemy have a chance to open fire on us in the middle of the river? We thought something strange must have happened. But this attack did not really endanger us.

"Then we landed in the water, which was knee-deep. We were fully armed with rifles and sabre and had our rucksacks on. We landed at about 12:50 a.m. The signal for a successful landing was red for the 18th Division."

—*Mitsuo Arai, master sergeant, 114th Regiment, 18th Division*

Right: Some youths organised the Overseas Chinese Guard Force and fought alongside the British forces.

Right: Under heavy Japanese shelling from the Johore shore, British forces failed to hold the line. By the dawn of February 9, the Japanese occupied the northwest shore of Singapore and pushed inland. They took Tengah Airfield in the evening.

Left: When the Jurong Line and Bukit Panjang Village fell on February 10, the British set alight the petrol depot behind Bukit Timah Village. It burned for 48 hours.

AFTERMATH OF BATTLE AT BUKIT TIMAH

"After we had passed the railway station [at 7th milestone Bukit Timah], perhaps quite near to the present Singapore Boys' Home, and behind which was a rubber plantation, we saw the British soldiers being killed while retreating into Holland Road. Their heads and legs were cut off, leaving only the torsos which were thrown into a drain. Some of the soldiers' hands were pierced through with wires and their bodies were slashed with swords into many linear wounds. They were stripped naked and with both their hands tied, were hung on trees by the Japanese.

"On our way home to 7th milestone [on February 15, 1942], we saw many dead bodies, mostly Indian soldiers, lying all over the place. Those soldiers might have been dead for two days. Their dead bodies were so swollen that they looked like water buffaloes. At least a few hundred Indian and British soldiers were killed behind the present Ngee Ann Polytechnic."

—*Lim Chok Fui, resident of Bukit Timah*

Left: On February 11, the Japanese took Bukit Timah. The British and local forces, backed by their heavy artillery, launched a counter-attack. A bloody hand-to-hand combat took place. The Japanese finally advanced towards the reservoir areas.

Right: From February 13 to 14, the Malay Regiment defending the Pasir Panjang Ridge fought heroically. Its C Company was almost completely annihilated by the Japanese. Annoyed by this strong resistance, the Japanese slaughtered the remaining captured Regiment men.

ALEXANDRA HOSPITAL MASSACRE

"We moved round the biscuits factory near Alexandra Hospital. They [the Japanese] went into the hospital at that time. And the next thing, we heard screams and noises, and we knew what was happening. We couldn't do anything about it. According to international law, you were not allowed to touch the hospitals. But the Japanese went into it. There was a Red Cross flag flying from the mast, and no way could they be mistaken. Even if they did not know, as soon as they entered the place, they must have realised it was a hospital. There was no mistake.

"The Japanese accused the British of firing from the hospital. But we were the only troops near to the hospital and I can assure you that we didn't fire from the hospital.

"[People] inside were massacred, didn't matter who it was – nursing staff, doctors, patients. [On February 16] we were allowed to send out five soldiers who volunteered to go and pick up the dead. We took one look inside, one ward, that's enough. The soldiers died of sword cuts, Japanese sword. We saw one chap, he wasn't dead, he had two cuts under his waist. He was groaning. So a Japanese soldier came along and killed him, in front of us."

—*Daniel Fraser, Royal Engineers*

Right: In view of losing all lines, including the reservoirs, Lieutenant General Percival went up to Upper Bukit Timah Road to meet Lieutenant General Yamashita on the evening of February 15, 1942.

Left and below: At 7:50 p.m. on February 15, the signing of the surrender document was concluded in the Ford factory at Upper Bukit Timah Road. This day was also the first day of the Chinese New Year.

Left: The rapidity with which Singapore fell to the Japanese was chronicled in verse by a British soldier:

Singapore, mighty fortress
Guardian of the East
The Japanese didn't think so
They took it in a week.

—"Pinkie" Evans, Manchester Regiment

Assembly of prisoners of war.

Prisoners of War

The old order ended on February 15, 1942 when the British surrendered to the Japanese Imperial Army. A new life had begun. Singapore was renamed Syonan-to, meaning "Light of the South". To many local Hokkiens it sounded like "Birdcage Island".

The stigma of defeat and the indignity of surrender weighed heavily on the soldiers of the British Empire. Though the fighting was over, an even greater challenge lay ahead for them. For the thousands of prisoners of war (POWs) who took the "long march" to internment, it was the beginning of the radical adjustments they would face in the days ahead. The last vestiges of the old order and the old way of life had dissolved.

The shock of filthy accommodation in the internment camp was often accompanied by the more immediate problem of food shortages. But order began to emerge out of this confusion. The POWs elected members to lead them and their own active involvement gave rise to a form of self-government in the camp.

Cooperation among the POWs to grow food, to supplement what the Japanese prison authorities provided, helped to foster camaraderie in suffering. When it became impossible to think of anything but food, the psychological effects must have been very distressing. However, hunger was not the only threat to a prisoner's morale. An even worse ordeal was isolation.

The internment camp government and some individual POWs initiated and organised activities which contributed enormously

---

Page 2   THE SYONAN TIMES, SATURDAY, FEBRUARY 21, 2602, SYOWA 17

DECLARATION

—OF THE—

COMMANDER OF THE NIPPON ARMY.

SINGAPORE is not only the connective pivot of the British Empire to control British India, Australia and East Asia, but the strong base to invade and squeeze them and Britain has boasted of its impregnable features for many years and it is generally accepted as an unsurmountable fortress.

Since the Nippon armies, however, have taken a military operation over the Malay Peninsula and Singapore, they have overwhelmed the whole peninsula within only two months and smashed the strong fort to pieces within 7 days and thus the British dominating power in British India, Australia and East Asia has collapsed in a moment and changed to, as if, a fan without a rivet or an umbrella without a handle.

Originally, the English has entertained extremely egoistic and dogmatic principles and they not only have despised others, but have been accustomed to carry out the free deceit, cunning and intimidation and they dared to commit the injus-

Above: A new chapter in the history of Singapore began with the proclamation of the New Japanese Order by Lieutenant General Tomoyuki Yamashita. The Japanese military authorities were confronted first and foremost with the task of how to deal with the 80,000 enemy soldiers and the 2,000 civilians to be interned.

Right: Changi Prison was initially where all civilian POWs were interned. It was originally built to hold a maximum of 600 convicts but eventually packed in over 3,000 POWs.

to camp morale. Amazingly rich programmes consisting of educational, cultural, recreational and religious activities became part of the fabric of the POW community.

But undoubtedly the most remarkable achievement of the POWs was the construction of the Siam-Burma Death Railway. Thousands died while working on it. The irony was that this railway, completed with such enormous suffering and loss of life, was operational for only a brief period. Like other projects built by the POW work parties, the Death Railway was destroyed before the return of the British.■

Left: Even children of the civilian POWs were interned with their parents. In September 1945, together with their parents, they celebrated freedom from captivity.

Right: Selarang Barracks. The military POWs of different armies were housed in separate barracks in Changi – Australians in Selarang, British and Dutch in Roberts and Indians in Kitchener.

SELARANG BARRACKS SQUARE INCIDENT

Four young POWs who tried to escape were recaptured by the Japanese and on August 30, 1942, all POWs in the Changi Barracks were ordered to sign the "No Escape Pledge." This was against the Geneva Convention on Prisoners of War which permitted opportunities to escape. The POWs refused to sign the document.

They were ordered to assemble in the Selarang Barracks Square area by the Japanese. A total of 15,400 men were crammed into an area which normally housed only 1,200. Food and sanitary conditions were very poor.

To force the POWs to sign, the four recaptured POWs were taken down to Changi beach and executed on September 2, 1942, with their senior officers watching.

The threat of an epidemic breaking out among the POWs living in an overcrowded area with poor sanitation gave the senior officers no choice but to ask their men to sign, with the understanding that they did so under duress.

On September 5, 1942, the signing took place and the POWs returned to their original barracks.

"So we signed. Many of us, of course, signed fictitiously. Oh yes, we did! I mean, instead of signing C.F. de Souza, I signed D.J. de Cruz or something like that. They wouldn't know because they couldn't check everyone, they didn't know who was who. So long as they got many forms back, they were quite happy."

—*Carl Francis de Souza, Straits Settlements Volunteer Corps*

Right: Selarang Barracks Square in September 1942, when the Australian POWs refused a Japanese military order to sign the "No Escape Pledge".

BARRACK SQ., SEPT., 1942.

Below: The execution of an Australian soldier.

Above: Each POW was given an identification badge.

Below: The Japanese incarcerated Indian POWs from the British Indian Army in concentration camps at Aljunied Road and Nee Soon. The photograph shows released Indian POWs in September 1945.

Right: In 1950, Elizabeth Choy received the Order of the British Empire (OBE) for her bravery during the war from Sir Patrick McKerron, governor of Singapore.

DOUBLE TENTH INCIDENT

On September 27, 1943, seven ships were destroyed in Keppel Harbour. The saboteurs escaped unnoticed.

The Japanese suspected that prisoners interned at Changi were not only receiving information over illicit wireless sets but also relaying information to Allied forces outside.

On October 10, 1943, the Japanese Military Police (*Kempeitai*) raided the cells in Changi Prison. Radio sets were seized. Fifty prisoners were interrogated. Fifteen died at the hands of their torturers.

"One day they put some bars of wood on the floor and they tied me up, and I had to kneel on this wood – very rough wood. And they stripped me topless. They tied me to the wood so that I couldn't go forward, I couldn't go backward, I couldn't go sideways, and they applied electric shock to me. And there my husband – they brought my husband – he was kneeling beside there watching me being tortured."

—Elizabeth Choy, canteen operator who was suspected of passing messages to POWs

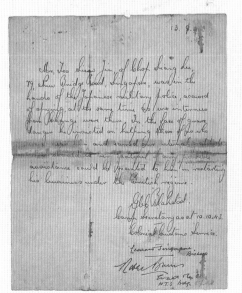

Left: Letter of gratitude, dated September 13, 1945, from the people who were helped by Teo Siew Jin during the "Double Tenth Incident".

Right: On May 1, 1944, all civilian POWs interned in Changi Prison were transferred to the Sime Road Camp. This was a move to make way for the 12,000 POWs from Selarang.

Above: Saint David's Church in the Sime Road Camp.

Left: British civilian POWs in the Sime Road Camp after the Japanese surrender.

Left: Not all civilian POWs were interned. Those who held positions of responsibility in essential services, for example engineers in the water and electricity departments, were identified by the "Civilian Enemy" armbands they were required to wear at work.

Opposite: It did not take the Japanese authorities too long to recognise the value of the POWs as a potential work force to help clean up the debris in the city and at the docks. They began to draw on POWs to form work parties and deployed them in various parts of the city.

Above: Prisoners who were members of work parties often took the opportunity to obtain or buy food from the local people, which they then smuggled into the camps. (Photograph taken after the Japanese surrender)

Right: Syonan Chureito, *or the Bukit Batok War Memorial at Upper Bukit Timah Road, was a project assigned to POW work parties. The shrine to commemorate fallen Japanese soldiers was unveiled amid much media publicity on September 10, 1942.*

Far right: Standing 10 feet (3 metres) high behind the Chureito *was the British War Memorial. The POWs were inspired to honour their comrades who had perished, and the Japanese military granted them permission to build their own monument.*

Above, right and below:
The construction of Syonan Jinja,
a Shinto shrine at MacRitchie
Reservoir, was another POW
work party project.

Towards the end of 1942, when the Japanese lost their command of the sea, land communication became important. The Japanese military decided to commence work on a railway line to link up Thailand and Burma (left), which was under their control. This was primarily to facilitate their efforts to expand into India.

Above and opposite: About 60,000 POWs from Japanese-occupied territories were sent to work on this railway line, the notorious "Death Railway". Later, civilian labourers were sent to speed up its construction. The death toll soon ran high as many died of malaria, cholera and dysentery due to the lack of medical attention.

DEATH RAILWAY – LIFE ON THE FRINGE

"Just before the gates of the camp of Kanburi [present-day Kanchanaburi], a prisoner of war collapsed and died. We were already suffering from the heat, blisters and hunger. We were all packed like sardines on the field with no shelter at all. The British officer in charge of the party told us in fact, 'I'll see if I can get you all a rest tomorrow.'

"The British officer at once went up to the Japanese and said, 'My men are not in a fit condition to march. They are all exhausted and have blisters on their feet, they must have some rest.'

"Then the Japanese said, 'Do you know I can have you shot for refusing to march?'

"We marched for three days, for some 50 miles [80 kilometres] along jungle tracks, through disease infested and insect ridden jungle. We were bitten by mosquitoes, insects and leeches. Our thirst was such that we drank from muddy pools. Our only food during the march was rice, tea or vegetable water.

"Many of us worked barefooted in the rain and sun. Even our clothes were worn out. And many were reduced to going about naked or with just a loincloth. Sometimes, they were lucky enough to obtain a rice bag and then they would use the rice bag."

—*Cleaver Rowell Eber, POW and Straits Settlements Volunteer (Eurasian Company)*

Above: Life as a POW was difficult. Major problems faced constantly were food, hygiene and overcrowding.

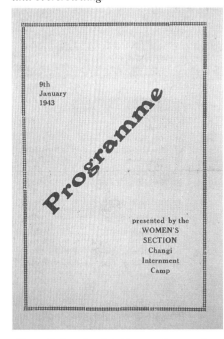

9th
January
1943

Programme

presented by the
WOMEN'S
SECTION
Changi
Internment
Camp

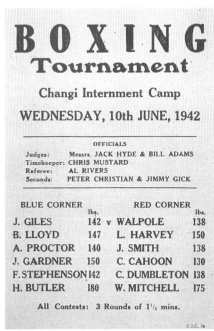

BOXING
Tournament

Changi Internment Camp

WEDNESDAY, 10th JUNE, 1942

OFFICIALS	
Judges:	Messrs. JACK HYDE & BILL ADAMS
Timekeeper:	CHRIS MUSTARD
Referee:	AL RIVERS
Seconds:	PETER CHRISTIAN & JIMMY GICK

BLUE CORNER	lbs.		RED CORNER	lbs.
J. GILES	142	v	WALPOLE	138
B. LLOYD	147		L. HARVEY	150
A. PROCTOR	140		J. SMITH	138
J. GARDNER	150		C. CAHOON	130
F. STEPHENSON	142		C. DUMBLETON	138
H. BUTLER	180		W. MITCHELL	175

All Contests: 3 Rounds of 1½ mins.

C.I.C. 70

Above (left and right): Despite the initial confusion and chaos of settling in in the internment camps, community life soon resumed as the POWs reorganised themselves. To boost their morale, they kept busy by arranging religious and social programmes such as concerts, drama performances and boxing tournaments.

Above: Classes on various subjects including Egyptology, mathematics, languages and history were taught, in what came to be called the University of Changi.

Right: Some POWs took the opportunity to do what they liked during their leisure time. Bombardier Stanley Warren spent his time sketching. This sketch shows exhausted troops arriving at the Sime Road transit camp from the southern coast of Johore.

MENTAL HEALTH

"I was worried by the fact that some of the prisoners just gazed into space and in the end it was easy for them to be in total emotional disorientation and they could become insane, you know.

"I thought it was a fight against insanity if you could really keep your mind occupied by having some sort of intellectual activity. You weren't sure what the long-term effect of imprisonment or malnutrition and disease would be.

"But at least I knew if I was going to survive, I was going to survive as a person, not as a vegetable."

—*Stanley Warren, POW, 135th Regiment*

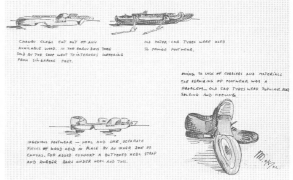

Above (left and right) and opposite: Another POW, W.R.M. Haxworth, a police officer, managed to execute some 800 paintings, sketches and cartoons, despite the shortage of paper. Most of his works depict the harsh living conditions in the camp, which he captured with great sensitivity and often with a slight touch of wry humour.

Right: Scraps of material were collected by the Girl Guides interned in Changi Prison, for their patchwork quilts.

BY THE TIME THE THIRD OCCUPANT OF THE CELL CAME IN THERE WAS VERY LITTLE SPACE TO SPARE. EXTRA BEDDING AND BAGS COMPLETED THE CONGESTION.

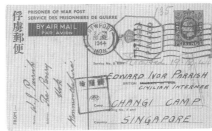

Above (top): Communication with the outside world was possible through the POW post.

Above (bottom): Essential medical care was provided by the POWs themselves. Blood group certificates were issued to the prisoners, showing that the POWs remained well organised within the encampment.

A mass-screening centre.

Sook Ching
(Purge through Purification)

To understand the Japanese policy towards the Chinese population in Malaya and Singapore one must go back to the Nanyang Chinese anti-Japanese sentiment which had been prevalent since the 1930s when Japan declared war on China. Local Chinese support for their compatriots in China saw the setting up of a China relief movement that included fund-raising campaigns, sending men and supplies for the war effort in China and boycotts of Japanese goods. Later, the fierce defence put up by the Chinese local resistance forces during the Japanese advance into Malaya deepened the resentment and suspicion of the Japanese against the local Chinese. As most of the officers of the 25th Army were veterans of the Sino-Japanese War, they also had a set of rather definite and fixed ideas about the Chinese community – that they should not be trusted and should be handled sternly. One of the reprisal acts of the Japanese military after the fall of Singapore was to carry out the *Sook Ching* (purge through purification) of the Chinese community.

Above: After the victory of the Japanese forces and the conquest of Singapore, the wrath of the Japanese Army fell upon the Chinese populace.

On the third day after Singapore surrendered, an order was given by the Japanese military to force all Chinese males to assemble at designated mass-screening centres. At several such centres, even women and children were reported to have been ordered to register themselves. What followed was an indiscriminate and bloody purge of the Chinese.

Many Singaporeans had no idea of what to expect when they were told to report to the respective areas of control. Tan Ban Cheng, a student during the Japanese Occupation, recalled in

MASS-SCREENING CENTRES AND KNOWN MASSACRE SITES

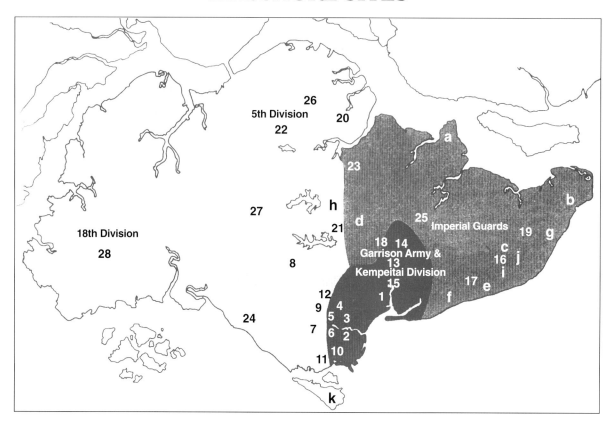

Above: On February 18, 1942, the General Headquarters of the 25th Army issued an order to launch the Sook Ching *operation to remove anti-Japanese elements within the Chinese population. The 25th Army divided the island into four sections and garrisoned them.*

Mass-screening Centres
1. North Bridge Road
2. Chinatown
3. Hill Street
4. Fort Canning
5. Great World Amusement Park
6. Pulau Saigon (near Robertson Quay)
7. Upper Cross Street
8. Tanglin Road
9. Tiong Bahru
10. Maxwell Road
11. Tanjong Pagar Road
12. Dhoby Ghaut
13. Jalan Sultan
14. Jalan Besar

15. Arab Street
16. Telok Kurau
17. Happy World Amusement Park
18. New World Amusement Park
19. Changi 10 ms
20. Punggol
21. Hougang 6 ms
22. Mandai 11 ms
23. Yio Chu Kang
24. Pasir Panjang
25. Upper Serangoon Road
26. Sembawang
27. Bukit Timah
28. Jurong

Known Massacre Sites
a. Ponggol Beach
b. Changi Beach/Changi Spit Beach – victims from Bukit Timah/Stevens Road *Sook Ching* point
c. Changi Road 8 ms 300 acre plantation (Samba Ikat village) – 250 victims from Changi 8 ms *Sook Ching* point
d. Hougang 8 ms – 6 lorryloads of people were said to have been massacred here
e. Katong 7 ms – 20 trenches were dug
f. Beach opposite 27 Amber Road – 2 lorryloads of people were said to have been massacred here; the site is now a car park
g. Tanah Merah Beach/Tanah Merah Besar Beach – 242 victims taken from Jalan Besar *Sook Ching* point; it is now a runway of Changi Airport
h. Thomson Road – Sime Road near golf course and the villages in the vicinity
i. Katong East Coast Road – 723 victims from Telok Kurau School *Sook Ching* point
j. Siglap area – Bedok South Avenue/Bedok South Road, previously known as Jalan Puay Poon
k. Blakang Mati Beach, off the Sentosa Golf Course, was a site where many bodies of the massacred victims were washed ashore and were buried.
    In addition, there were also claims that people were massacred at places like the East Coast Road 10 ms and 3/4 ms, Tanjong Pagar Harbour Board area and Bukit Timah 6 ms Namly area. The killing at Namly area was believed to have taken place even before the *Sook Ching* operation.

his oral history interview that "we did not know exactly what was the idea of the whole exercise. It was only after the event when we heard of people missing that we had an idea that they might be picking up some of these people, thinking that they might have resisted them or be potentially able to resist them."

A most terrifying feature of the *Sook Ching*, well remembered by most people, was the "identification parade". People were made to pass in single file before a row of hooded informers. A nod of the head from any one of these hooded informers signified recognition and the victim was immediately picked out and sent to a detention room. Most people who were picked up for questioning were never seen again. Chinese suspects were loaded onto lorries and driven away to killing grounds where they were machine-gunned and bayoneted. Many people disappeared without a trace. Today, the number of Chinese massacred during the *Sook Ching* is an issue of much speculation and controversy. The *Sook Ching* marked an important point in Japanese military relations with the Chinese community – the brutal purge was to drive many Chinese into the arms of the communist-dominated guerillas.■

Above: Notices were put up to inform Chinese males between the ages of 18 and 50 to report to various mass-screening centres for inspection. The people were notified through loudspeakers, by Japanese soldiers or by word of mouth.

Top: In certain mass-screening centres, such as Jalan Besar and Jalan Sultan, women and children were also screened, although the Japanese were mainly after men. Some people were told to bring three to five days' supply of food. The less fortunate went without food or drinking water for days.

Bottom: Mass-screening centre at Tanjong Pagar Police Station. It was said that people detained at the Tanjong Pagar and Tiong Bahru areas were executed at sea near Blakang Mati Island (present-day Sentosa).

MASS SCREENING – LIFE ON THE LINE

"We just sat on the [school] field and waited, just hung around and waited until daylight. I think the whole purpose of the exercise was that they were after communists. And they went about it in their own strange fashion.

"In some areas, as I was told, there were interviews. We were not interviewed at all and from the moment we entered the field, except for the Japanese soldiers, nobody cared a hoot for us. Nobody bothered us right until we left. Nobody bothered with us at all, which was a strange thing because if you are after communists, I would have thought that the first group of people you would want to go after would be students. That was another reason why I say, we were lucky.

"They started to sort us out. They made an announcement and said they want to separate us. Firstly, they called for merchants and towkays. Now, how do you identify a towkay? Whether you regard yourself a towkay is entirely up to you. If you think you are a towkay, you stepped out. They lined them up and took them to some place. Then they called for government servants, people in the civil service. So all the civil servants came out. Hawkers, they categorised them into various occupations. Until they came to our turn and asked for students, college and school students."

—*Lee Kip Lin, student screened at Telok Kurau Mass-Screening Centre*

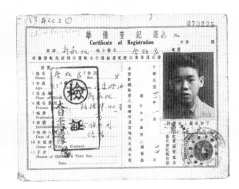

Right: This illustration of the brutal killing of the local people taken from a mass-screening centre was drawn by renowned Singapore artist Liu Kang after the Japanese surrender.

IMPACT OF *SOOK CHING*

"The impact of war on us was very great. My father was taken away during the *Sook Ching*. If my father was with us, our life would be very wonderful. We would have the opportunity to study. I had about one year education after the war and had to stop schooling – my elder sister and I. It affected my whole family greatly. My mother lost my father."

—*Foo Hee Hong, housewife*

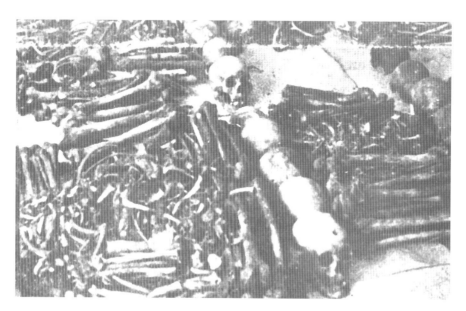

Left: Those who were taken away from the mass-screening centres were herded onto lorries and driven en masse to be massacred in remote parts of the island, such as Changi, Punggol and Bedok. Some burial grounds at these sites were found only after the war. At the War Crimes Trial in 1947, the Japanese defendants admitted to killing 5,000 Chinese civilians, although the figure quoted by the local sources stood at 50,000.

Right: Although the number of Chinese killed was the largest, other races who did not cooperate with the Japanese military authorities were not spared. Sikh soldiers who cooperated with the British were also shot by Japanese soldiers.

ESCAPE FROM THE TRENCH OF DEATH

"They [the Japanese] took us to Bedok. There was a hill where they had pillboxes facing the sea. They had three or four trenches there. But before we were taken down to that place, they took all our belongings – pen, watches, everything they took. There were about 90 of us. We were tied with our hands behind our backs. Then we were put on the lorries. But when we alighted from the lorry, we were still with our hands behind our backs. In the open, they pushed us down to the trench and they asked us to stand.

"Everyone was scared and don't know what would happen. But most of us thought that we were going to die already, they were going to shoot us.

"The order came and then they just shoot. Bang! The second time they shot, bang! up to about three times. So all those who died would fall down. I was hit on my knee. Suddenly, I remember that I am still alive. So when the first man dropped dead, I followed him. Then the third man covered me on top.

"To make sure all were dead, they gave a third fire. Another ten rounds, bomp-bomp-bomp, like that, finished. Then they had no time so they just covered the trench with planks. And then they went to the next group. They finished the whole thing in about 20 minutes' time. Everything ended."

—*Chan Cheng Yean, massacre survivor, Malacca Volunteer Corps*

Tanjong Pagar Railway Station, renamed Syonan Railway Station.

Japanese Military Administration

Like other Japanese-occupied territories in Southeast Asia, Singapore was to be administered by a military government. The Japanese Military Administration for Malaya and Singapore was set up in March 1942. While the Malayan states were organised into provinces, with a chief administrator appointed for each province, Singapore was created as a special Municipality or *Tokubetsu Si*. At the helm of the Municipality was a mayor who was the head of the civil administration.

In the Japanese administrative structure, the military wielded supreme power. Governing the occupied areas was exclusively a military undertaking. Executive power was concentrated in the hands of the military which was reluctant to delegate authority to civil bureaucrats. Consequently, there was, in the words of Professor Yoji Akashi, a Japanese historian, "... a jam in the administrative process and a slowdown in policy making."

From the start of Japanese rule in Malaya, the *Gunseikanbu* (military administration) was split into two feuding factions – the *Watanabe Gunsei* (April 1942 to March 1943) and the *Odachi* faction (Shigeo Odachi was the first mayor of the Syonan Municipality, from February 1942 to July 1943). Hostility between the two factions was caused by disagreements over fundamentals of administrative philosophy and methods of implementing policies. Each faction set out to obstruct and undermine the other.

Rivalry and sectionalism at every level of the Japanese Military Government influenced its operation to the detriment of the

Above: The General Headquarters of the Southern Expeditionary Forces (GHSEF), which was responsible for the invasion and administration of South Asia, came under the supreme command of Count Hisaichi Terauchi (right). In March 1943, the GHSEF moved from Saigon to Singapore and was located at the Singapore Governor's Residence (now the Istana). Premier Tojo (left) visited Singapore in 1943.

Left: The headquarters of the Gunseikanbu *(Japanese Military Administration) was in Fullerton Building. Its primary concern was to strengthen the power of the Japanese military by extracting from the occupied territories resources vital for imperialistic expansion.*

Below: Singapore was governed by the Japanese Military Administration. This was dominated by field grade officers from the General Affairs Department, which was at the bottom of the military administration structure. Wataru Watanabe was the first chief of the General Affairs Department (March 1942 to March 1943). He represented the hardline faction, whose harsh and unpopular policies were soon a common practice.

administration and welfare of the occupied areas. The power rivalry between the General Headquarters of the Southern Expeditionary Forces (GHSEF) and the 25th Army was a case in point. With the transfer of the 25th Army from Singapore to Sumatra, Malaya came under the command of the *Gunseikanbu* in Sumatra in 1943. The reassignment of the army command and changes in personnel in the military hierarchy, coupled with differences in the conditions of these two territories, did not contribute to a stable and cohesive administration. There was a change of the seat of power in April 1944 when the GHSEF moved to Manila and later transferred to Saigon. In the meantime, the 7th Area Army was responsible for the administration of Malaya until the surrender of the Japanese in 1945.

While the power struggles continued, the economy was disrupted and people's lives continued to be shattered. The locals were not the only ones who suffered. The Japanese Occupation in Singapore also had a profound impact on foreign workers. The treatment of Indonesian labourers who were brought in as forced labour and the infamous exploitation of "comfort women" are reminders of the savagery of Japanese military rule.

In the absence of administrative continuity and the failure of the bureaucracy to provide a system of efficient government, the Japanese Military Administration lost the opportunity to win the hearts and minds of the people. ■

STRUCTURE OF THE JAPANESE MILITARY ADMINISTRATION

*Supreme Commander
Southern Forces*
Hisaichi Terauchi

*Commander
(Malaya & Sumatra)*
Tomoyuki Yamashita

*Superintendent of Military
Administration*
Sosaku Suzuki

Departments	Investigation & Research Agency	Auxiliary Bureaus	Governors	Mayors

- General Affairs
- International Affairs
- Police Affairs
- Judiciary
- Financial Affairs
- Industrial Affairs
- Communications
- Sanitation
- Propaganda
- Accounts

- Railways
- Correspondence
- Shipping
- Enemy Property Control
- Broadcasting

Above: The administration of Malaya, which included Singapore and Sumatra, was in the hands of the 25th Army of the Southern Expeditionary Forces under Lieutenant General Yamashita. However, power struggles and rivalry between the GHSEF and the 25th Army resulted in the reassignment of Yamashita and the 25th Army from Singapore to Sumatra in June 1942 and March 1943 respectively.

Right: The 7th Army was responsible for the administration of Malaya from January 1944. Moderate policies were adopted during this period. Seishiro Itagaki headed this army for a brief period, from April 1945 until the Japanese surrender.

Right: Indigenous people of the Japanese-occupied territories were mobilised to clear the war debris and rebuild the island. In Singapore, the Japanese military brought in some 1,700 coolies from Java as forced labourers and housed them at a camp in Seletar.

INDONESIAN LABOURERS

"I was asked to accompany an officer to go and visit an Indonesian camp at Henderson Road just before reaching Depot Road. But there were quite a number of sick patients there. I understand, some of them were actually still undergraduates. So they were actually being brought here under the pretext that they would be given a job. There were also quite a number of Indonesian girls … so they were brought here to entertain the [Japanese] officers. So they, too, had been bluffed.

"They [Indonesian labourers] were given rice. But then probably not enough. So the Indonesians wanted to go out. At first, they were arrested and brought back to the camp. But I think, later, they [the Japanese] simply allowed them [to go], probably because they could not get enough food to feed them.

"So that was why we found a lot of them out on this Kandang Kerbau Road. Some were even living under the Kandang Kerbau bridge, where they made their homes. So they were just like scavengers, going round begging for food or going through the dustbins to look for food."

—*Chin Sin Chong, student employed at* 15848 Butai

Left: Many of these coolies were very badly treated. Most of them suffered from beri-beri or dysentery.

Right: Besides forced labour, one of the ominous policies of the Japanese Military Administration was the wartime exploitation of women, mostly Koreans. They provided sexual services and an emotional outlet to relieve the combat tension of the Japanese soldiers. This photograph, taken in the Andaman Islands on October 12, 1945, shows women brought from Malaya who were coerced to become "comfort women".

KOREAN COMFORT WOMEN IN BLAKANG MATI

"Some of the girls told me, with tears running down their cheeks, that in Korea, at first they were asked to work in some restaurants for the Japanese in Singapore … and they were sent to the island of Singapore. However, on this island [Blakang Mati or Sentosa], they were forced to become prostitutes for the Japanese Army.

"They told me their stories in tears. The head of the Japanese unit was a Lieutenant Miki who was a very bad man. Before the girls were distributed to the other soldiers, he 'tasted' one by one every night. I believe they were all virgins.

"In the army there were five or six young boys, about 15 to 16 years of age, and they were working with the civilian administration. One day, I discovered one of the boys hiding at one corner crying very heartily. I asked him if he was homesick. He told me that Lieutenant Miki, while forcing himself on the girls, had forced him to help. After hearing that, I was very shocked. I asked myself: 'How could the Japanese behave this way?' There was not even the slightest regard to someone's dignity. I started to hate this military structure."

—*Fujiwara Takashi (Nagase Takashi), army translator*

STRUCTURE OF SYONAN MUNICIPALITY
(Tokubetsu Si)

```
                              MAYOR
    ┌──────────┬──────────┬──────────┬──────────┐
 General    Bureau of   Economic   Undertaking   Police
 Affairs    Welfare     Bureau     Bureau        Bureau
```

General Affairs	Bureau of Welfare	Economic Bureau	Undertaking Bureau	Police Bureau
Secretariat	Promotion of Well-being of the People	Commerce	Engineering	Police Affairs
Accounts	Education	Food Control	Water	Peace
Treasury	Medical	Agriculture	Electrical	Criminal
Revenue	Health		Gas	Special Branch
Superintendents	Town Cleansing		Traffic	
Custodian of Enemy Property				

Above: City Hall housed the offices of the Syonan Municipality. Rivalry between the military and the civil bureaucracy was the most serious problem in the Japanese administration.

Malai Inspection Party Leaves For Bahau

A PARTY of ten representatives of the newly-formed Malai Welfare Association, Syonan, left on Monday for Serting Hilir in Bahau, Negri Sembilan, to make a preliminary survey of the area which is being allotted to Syonan Malais who are desirous of taking up farming, Domei reports.

The party's departure was the result of a Committee meeting held on Dec. 31 of all members of the Malai Welfare Association here.

The group, which left was headed by the President of the Malai Welfare Association, Tengku Kader, others being Omar Othman, Zaimal Abidin Ahmad, Ibrahm Ali, Haji Abdullah, Haji Idris, Mohamed Isa, Ahmad Sa'id, Yasin Kulsb, and Zubir Salam. Robert Koh, Chinese cameraman attached to the Malai Press, also accompanied the group.

Enquiries reveal that the party will probably stay in Bahau for about a week. It is understood that Malai farmers residing in Syonan who are desirous of availing themselves of the splendid opportunity offered by Government to emigrate to Bahau to cultivate the land, are now registering themselves at the headquarters of the Malai Welfare Association.

Left: The Malays and Arabs also had their own respective welfare associations.

Below: Deterioration of the Japanese position in the war compelled the Japanese to re-evaluate their stand of absolute power. To win the hearts and minds of the people, some form of political participation by the locals was encouraged. The Syonan Advisory Council was formed on December 7, 1943 with the mayor of the Tokubetsu Si as the chairman. The Council's 15 members represented the various racial groups. Among them were Ching Kee Sun, Haji Siraj, A. Yellapa, M.V. Pillai, S.M. Alkaff and Dr C.J. Paglar.

Group photo of Kempeitai
(Military Police).

Law and Order

The immediate task to restore law and order fell to the Japanese Military Police or *Kempeitai*. For most people the mention of "*Kempeitai*" was synonymous with fear and hatred.

Looting was rampant at the beginning of the Japanese Occupation. The Japanese authorities adopted severe remedies, including beheading the looters they caught and displaying the heads for public viewing. This was intended to serve as a warning to the rest of the population.

Three days after the fall of Singapore, the Japanese military authorities ordered the mass screening of the Chinese community. Yamashita and his staff had decided it was extremely important to ferret out anti-Japanese elements among the Chinese community and to punish them, especially since the strength of the 25th Army had been considerably weakened by the Malayan campaign. Besides the massive screening operation, on a daily basis, the Japanese had spies who permeated every walk of life.

The *Kempeitai* and the police maintained constant vigilance over the people. They also used the *jikeidan* (auxiliary police system) to keep tabs on people's movements. Again, as for the Overseas Chinese Association and Eurasian Welfare Association, the same concept of using prominent figures, in this case prominent neighbourhood figures, was implemented. It is not hard to imagine that some of them were faced with the same dilemma which confronted the community leaders of the OCA and the Eurasian Welfare Association, in that they were working

Above: Plainclothes Japanese Kempeitai *were assigned to mingle with the people in early 1942.*

for the Japanese authorities. The response of the local population towards these community leaders is best summed up by this excerpt from Gay Wan Guay's oral history interview:

"In some cases, I believe some of them were disliked very much because it was quite obvious they did get certain privileges. But others were doing the duty out of pressure and did not take advantage of it. So we understood the situation. It depended on the individual carrying out the duty. You know, some people could be very overbearing, the more you gave them authority. Of such people … when the British came back, they had justice meted out on them in one way or another." ■

Above: A special police unit, known as Tokkeitai, *which consisted of some 50 military policemen, came under the command of First Lieutenant (later Major) Satoru Onishi (circled in the photograph). His mission was to conduct counter-communist operations in Malaya and Singapore.*

Above: The Kempeitai *exercised complete powers of arrest and interrogation. Torture often came before investigation. Common modes used were the infamous "water" and "fire" treatments. These inhumane treatments were meant to break the toughest resistance.*
Right: Whipping was another common torture used by the Kempeitai. *Offenders were left suspended upside down to be whipped. This illustration is taken from Liu Kang's booklet "Chop Suey".*
Below right: Lim Seng, a civilian POW, was given the "water" treatment after his arrest by the Kempeitai. *This photograph was taken upon his release from Outram Jail in September 1945.*

WATER TORTURE

"They forced water down my throat until my belly bloated. They then tied me to the ladder, and let go. Two persons carried me and threw me into the airwell. With their foot on my chest, they trampled hard on it. Water just gushed out. After I regained consciousness, I was sent back to my cell. On the following day, the same whole process of torture was repeated.

"I lost a lot of weight due to the psychological effects. Very serious. It was not good to have water forced down, your health would be affected.

"During the period when I was terribly tortured, I dreamt someone who told me this: 'You must admit, or else they [the Japanese] would beat you to death.' I replied: 'I did nothing wrong.' The answer came back as: 'Even if you have not, you must still admit you're wrong.'

"The next day when I was taken out to be tortured again, I admitted and for that day, I did not receive the water treatment."

—*Lim Seng, civilian POW*

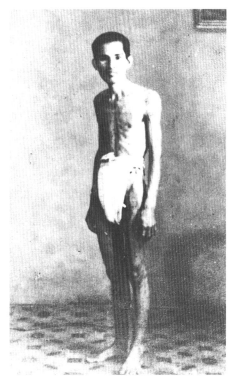

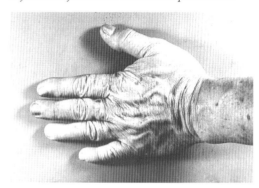

Left and below: Sometimes, to induce a confession, suspects' nails were clamped. Traces of such torture remain forever. (Illustration from Liu Kang's booklet "Chop Suey".) The twisted index finger in the photograph below shows that deformities from such torture are permanent.

FEAR OF THE *KEMPEITAI*

"People would be wondering when is my turn coming for the *Kempeitai* to come and take me away. All someone needs to do is to spread a false rumour or talk something about somebody and the *Kempeitai* would look out for that individual and say oh, you are pro-British, pro-American or pro-Nationalist China … or you are a communist or you are a blackmarketeer. They would accuse of anything and they could just come and take you away for questioning and detain you indefinitely."

—*Soon Kim Seng, storekeeper*

Above left: The YMCA at Stamford Road was the Kempeitai *East District Branch.*
Above right: The Kempeitai *West District Branch was in a private residence at Smith Street.*

Right: The Central Police Station in South Bridge Road was another Kempeitai *branch.*

Below: Crime was negligible during the Japanese Occupation because punishment for even the pettiest crime was most severe. The public display of the heads of looters in places like Dhoby Ghaut and Kallang Bridge frightened many people into submission after the fall of Singapore.

DECAPITATION

"When the Japanese came in, during the first fortnight, they beheaded eight people and their heads were put into iron cages, and hung up at eight different places. The notices put beside the heads read: 'These eight people were beheaded because they disobeyed the law of the Imperial Japanese Army.' They were accused of looting, misbehaviour and belonging to different gangster groups. The notices spelt out that anyone caught in these acts would be given the same treatment."

—*Neoh Teik Hong, clerk*

Right: Japanese sentry at Elgin Bridge. Sentry posts were set up at every street corner. For fear of Japanese inspection, most people carried whatever identification papers they had at all times.

SLAPPED BY THE JAPANESE

"I detested the Japanese because I was often bullied by them when they came here. Our shop was at Cecil Street. I was beaten up by them a few times at the bridge. I disliked all the Japanese who I met. I was bullied by them too many times.

"There was once when I was riding on my bicycle to Cecil Street and halfway I met a Japanese whose bicycle had broken down. He gave his bicycle to me and took away my bicycle. Moreover, he also slapped me on the face. How unreasonable was he? Not only did he take my bicycle, but I was also slapped by him!"

—Liau Thai Chuan, civilian

Left: Bowing to a sentry on duty was considered an expression of deep respect for the Japanese soldier. Civilians had to perform this act of homage on reaching a checkpoint.

Left and far left: In April 1942, the police initiated the registration of families. Police representatives visited every home to register all occupants, who were then issued a "Peace Living Certificate" or Ankyosho, recognising them as "proper residents."

Below left: By April 1943, the Ankyosho was replaced by a "Census Taking List." Copies of the list were kept at police stations. Surprise checks by the police were often made on households. Any changes in the household, in cases of birth, death or change of address, had to be reported to the police.

Below right: An auxiliary police system (APS) was introduced in September 1942. Well-known civilians in the area were pressed into serving in the APS. Their appointment letters were issued by the police stations.

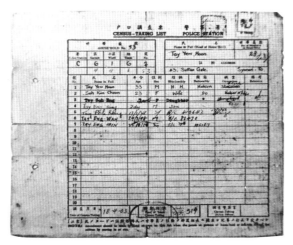

Left: APS Badges
6 – The auxiliary police assistant, also known as a three-star man, was in charge of 3,000 households.
22 – The head of a ward, also known as a two-star man, was in charge of 300 households.
25 – The head of a team, also known as a one-star man, was in charge of 30 households.

Left: APS badge and armband of the head of a team. The duty of the auxiliary police was to assist the police in the preservation of law and order and to report the presence of suspicious characters. They were also required to bring shortages of foodstuff to the notice of the authorities.

AUXILIARY POLICE SYSTEM

"At the beginning was only family registration. You see, whatever they want to know, they'll just ask. Or whatever they want us to let the people know what the government wants, they just let us know and we will inform them. I think it's a go-between work. We have actually no power, unlike the police who could arrest people. Our job was just to give information and to collect information.

"Sometimes, they wanted to know what this family is doing – were there bad hats or not. They asked us to investigate. Of course if they informed me, I'd have to find out under which two-star man and tell the two-star man about it – that they [the Japanese] wanted some information about this family. The two-star man would help the one-star man. The one-star man was supposed to know all the 30 families very well. So the two-star man could get information from the one-star man. And then we submit what we know."

—*Tan Wah Meng, three-star man*

Left: In June 1944, as the war situation deteriorated against Japan, night patrol was enforced to increase vigilance over public order. A night patrol notice was issued to all males aged between 16 and 45, to perform such duty in two shifts through the night, from 11 p.m. to 7 a.m.

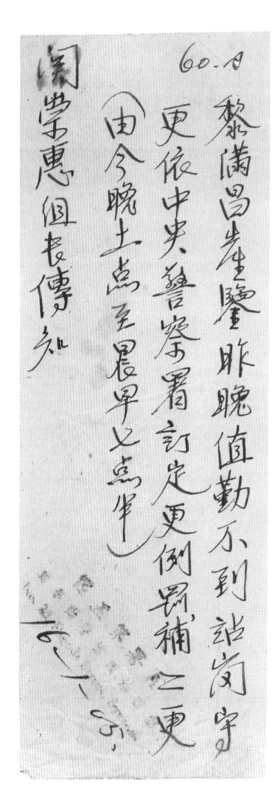

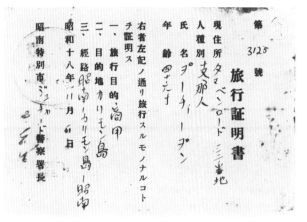

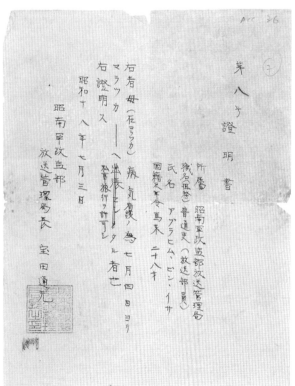

Left: Persons who failed to report for night patrol duty at the stipulated shift time had to make up time. As a penalty they were allotted the second shift.

Above: Passes for travel outside Singapore could be obtained from the police station (top) or the government department where one worked. This allowed the Japanese authorities to monitor people's movements closely. These two travel passes were issued by the police station and the Broadcasting Bureau (bottom) in 1943.

Japanese propaganda publications.

Battle for the Hearts and Minds

For the people of Singapore, after the fall of the island, what lay ahead was a time of rapid adjustment to the Japanese regime. The Japanese set about wiping out all traces of the West and embarked upon the promotion of the Greater East Asia Co-Prosperity Sphere, where the ultimate vision was to achieve one Asian race, culture and language.

The "superior culture" of Japan was espoused as a model for the progress of all Japanese-occupied territories. To achieve their aims, the Japanese attempted to unite themselves with the people they had conquered by first bridging the communication gap. They introduced a lingua franca, *Nippon-go*, which was intended to serve as the epitome of the new Asian solidarity.

Concurrently they launched a campaign of Nipponisation. To supplement Japanese language instruction, the authorities encouraged the teaching of Japanese customs, manners and songs, and screened Japanese films. It is difficult to gauge the success of learning *Nippon-go* over the three and a half years of Japanese Occupation, or how effectively during the process, the Japanese spirit, or *Nippon seishin*, was transmitted to the people.

To the small number of people who either worked for the Japanese or whose occupation required a knowledge of *Nippon-go*, there were sufficient economic reasons to induce them to

Above: Publications came under the strict control of the Propaganda Department. Ideologies such as "The Greater East Asia Co-Prosperity Sphere", "Hakko Ichiu" (Universal Brotherhood) and the "superior culture" of Japan were advocated.

Right: The propaganda machinery of the Japanese Military Administration was driven by the Propaganda Department. This department, located in the Cathay Building, controlled all publications, periodicals, newspapers, films, broadcasts and amusement grounds.

learn. For the rest of the population, there was little reason to learn *Nippon-go* beyond the basic salutations.

If one were asked to identify the single biggest setback Japan faced in carrying out her propaganda campaign, the answer must be the simple fact that Japan was a nation at war. Shortages of qualified language teachers and teaching materials did not help improve the situation. The endeavour to Nipponise the local population was thwarted by the short period of rule which did not allow the Japanese language policy to seep in and entrench itself in the lives of the local people.■

THE SYONAN TIMES

No. 3   SUNDAY, FEBRUARY 22, 2602, SYOWA 17   5 cents

BRILLIANT NIPPON SUCCESSES

Air Force Deals Death Blow To Port Darwin

Loss Of Bases Puts Allies On Verge Of Total Collapse

Secret Of Nippon Successes

Berlin, Feb. 21.

THE secret of Nipponese successes ever since the outbreak of the war in East Asia is the spiritual strength of the Nipponese people, comments a leading German newspaper published here.

Timor Island Landing

AUSTRALIAN CIRCLES SHOCKED

Lisbon, Feb. 21.

BOTH official circles and the

Left and opposite top: All newspapers in Singapore were employed in the Japanese war propaganda.

The Syonan Sinbun

[ENGLISH Edition]

No. 51   TUESDAY, FEBRUARY 9, KOKI 2603, SYOWA 18   7 Cents.

'Nippon Will Treat East Asia Peoples As Brothers, Sisters'

Premier Tojo's Declaration At Lower House Meeting
'HAKKO ICHIU' STRESSED

Domei.

TOKYO, Feb. 9.—Premier General Hideki Tojo declared yesterday before a hearing of the Lower House Budget Committee that Nippon must and will treat all peoples in the Greater East Asia Co Prosperity Sphere as true brothers and sisters, and expressed his firm confidence that, by so doing they will come to understand the true meaning of "Hakko Ichiu," the principle founding the Empire of Nippon.

The statement was made in the course of a reply to an interpellation by the representative of Hyogo Prefecture, concerning the guiding principle for economic development of the Southern Regions.

The Premier said: "The guiding conception for economic development of Greater East Asia is to be found in the principle issuing the Nippon Empire. Of course, it would be difficult to make other nationals thoroughly comprehend the principle in a day. But I feel confident that if we persistently strive towards this end, they will come to understand it.

"The object of the establishment of the Greater East Asian Affairs Ministry also lies in this aim. I am inclined to think that with the outbreak of the War of Greater East Asia, all nations within the Greater East Asia Co-Prosperity Sphere have realised the true aim of Nippon.

"Therefore, we must and will treat them as our brothers and sisters as set forth in the Imperial Rescript for Education.

"To extend your benevolence to all and you cannot err in all ages. I shall make the best endeavours toward that end," the Premier said.

Diet Continues Work Smoothly And Swiftly

Domei.

TOKYO, Feb. 8.—With the Imperial Diet working swiftly and smoothly, all bills which have been submitted by the Government...

Burmese Cheer Tojo's Statement

The people of Burma are seen overwhelmed with joy by the declaration of Premier Tojo that Burma is to become an independent state within this year.—(Domei photo).

Two Fighter Planes Donated To Navy

Domei.

TSINGTAO, Feb. 7.—Two fighter planes have been donated to the Imperial Nippon naval forces by members of various cotton textile companies here.

It will be recalled that two bombers have already been presented to the Navy by Nippon residents here.

German Tanks Launch Fierce Attacks On Eastern Front
U-BOATS SINK MORE ALLIED SHIPS

Domei.

LISBON, Feb. 7.—Numerous attacks by German tanks featured the operations on the Eastern Front on Saturday, as a result of which the Reich forces have re-established important connections between German advanced bases and main German positions, according to latest dispatches received.

Reliable German sources in Berlin say that these attacks were launched from important centres with great fierceness, and in many cases Soviet formations deployed for the attack were dispersed.

German Stukas, bombers and fighters were employed all day long...

Measures Being Discussed For Internees' Relief

Domei.

TOKYO, Feb. 8.—With a view...

NIPPON BOMBERS RAID KWEILIN AND HENGYANG

Heavy Damage Inflicted On Military Facilities

Domei.

UNDISCLOSED BASE, Feb. 8.—In the face of unfavourable flying weather, a combined unit of Nippon Army bombers and fighters this morning raided the enemy air base in Kweilin, capital of Kwangsi Province, inflicting heavy damage on enemy military facilities, including the wireless station.

Close on the heels of the morning raid another formation of Nippon Army planes late this afternoon attacked Kweilin again, bombing and damaging military establishments.

Simultaneous with the second raid on Kweilin, another Nippon combined air unit of bombers and fighters made a surprise attack on Hengyang, in the central part of Hunan Province, and bombed the enemy air base and other military facilities, inflicting heavy damages.

All Nippon planes returned to their bases safely, despite the heavy anti-aircraft fire from enemy guns.

Cameraman Reveals Sad Plight Of Chungking

Domei.

SHANGHAI, Feb. 8.—A detailed account of present conditions in Chungking was given here by Chang Hung-tang, a leading cameraman and film technician in China, who took advantage of his assignment to Hongkong the outset of the Greater East Asia War to escape from Chungking.

Chang, who joined Wong Ching-wei's regime, is now happily working for the China Film Company in Shanghai, his home town.

He revealed that during his two...

U.S. Policy Based On Self-Interest

Domei.

LISBON, Feb. 7.—It is reported from Washington, Under Secretary of State Sumner Welles, in a speech at the University of Maryland on Feb. 5, declared the foreign policy of the United States must be based on what Americans believed to be "their practical self-interest and not on emotional altruism of sentimental aspiration."

Political observers here declared a statement of this sort from one who holds a high position in United States foreign policy-making organ is highly significant in view of the repeated cry for material aid from Chungking and the Soviet Union.

U.S. Citizens Warned To Tighten Belts

Domei.

LISBON, Feb. 8.—The Times correspondent reported from Washington on Feb. 5 that Claude Wickard, United States Secretary of Agriculture, has declared that Americans must tighten their belts in the coming year in order to make food available for the United States Army and for other...

Tenno Heika Grants Sacred Treasure Order

Domei.

TOKYO, Feb. 8.—Tenno Heika today conferred on Sutharm Phiphit Sali of Tokyo, former Vice-President of Nippon-Thai Society, the third class Order of the Sacred Treasure in recognition of his services for the promotion of friendly relations between Nippon and Thailand.

Heroic Exploits Earn Sakai Unit War Citation
OPERATIONS IN CENTRAL CHINA

Domei.

TOKYO, Feb. 8.—The War Ministry announced that the exploits of the Sakai Corps and other co-operating corps in exterminating the enemy in the mountains of Chekiang and Kiangsi Provinces, central China, last May, have been brought to the attention of Tenno Heika.

It will be recalled the Sakai Corps carried the remains of their commander, Lieut. Gen. Naoji Sakai, throughout the operations until the enemy had been encircled and completely annihilated.

The Corps later received citation from the district commander.

The announcement of the War Ministry follows: "The Sakai Corps and other corps attached to it, which received citation from the district commander for their valorous deeds in Chekiang and Kiangsi Provinces, have now been brought to the attention of Tenno Heika.

"When operations started in Chekiang and Kiangsi Provinces during the middle part of May last year, the Corps under the command of Lieut. Gen. Naoji Sakai, advanced to Lanchi, a strategic enemy city on the Kinkwa-Lanchi front, and after exterminating the enemy in the surrounding mountains, occupied the city on May 27.

Left and below: There was not much real news in the military-controlled newspapers, but people needed to read them for the announcements which sometimes had a life-or-death relevance for them.

SYONAN TOKUBETU-SI NOTICE No. 70

CHANGE OF ADDRESS MUST BE REPORTED.

The public is hereby informed that registered families must report at their Police Divisional Headquarters, where they first registered, of any change of address or any other particulars in the Ankyosyo. Failure to comply with this order will be severely dealt with.

MAYOR,
SYONAN TOKUBETU-SI.

Dated June 1, 2602.

105-111

M. A. D. NOTICE No. 3

Compulsory Inoculation Against Typhoid Fever.

Compulsory inoculation against typhoid fever will be instituted for all persons in Syonan-to commencing on Friday 27th February, 2602.

Any person who can produce evidence of having been successfully inoculated during the past year and infants under two years of age need not be inoculated.

The inoculations will be carried out district by district at selected centres, the sites of which and the corresponding dates to be notified later. The inoculations will be carried out at the centres between the hours of 8.30 a.m. and 4.00 p.m.

Inoculations will also be carried out at existing First Aid Posts and Dispensaries for the benefit of persons who live near these places.

Any person who fails to receive inoculation without proper reason shall be punished.

THE COMMANDING OFFICER,
THE MILITARY ADMINISTRATION DEPT.

Dated, Syonan-to, February 24th, 2602.

Above: To pursue their policy of Nipponisation, the Japanese authorities organised street exhibitions with slogans calling for "unity and strengthening" of Japan with the people of Singapore. These were meant to imbue the populace with the Japanese spirit.

Above (left and right): An important section of the Propaganda Department was the Syonan Central Broadcasting Station or Hosokyoku. Japanese songs such as "Patriotic March" (Aikoku Koshiukyoku) and "Song of the Decisive War of Greater East Asia" (Daitoa Kessen No Uta) over the air waves were meant to propagate a Japanese ethos.

Left: Comics were used to ridicule the West. Japanese-inspired comics also sought to discredit the strength of the Allied forces.

Right and below: Kamishibai *or picture/ storycard shows were a form of propaganda cum entertainment frequently employed by the Japanese authorities. Local artists were recruited to work at the Syonan Kamishibai Production Centre in Orchard Road.*

PROPAGANDA

"Before the actual movie, they had a sort of propaganda film – *Asia is for Asians*. And then they showed you newsreels of Japanese military forces in action. All this while they would be showing you they were winning everywhere. For certain parts, they would show you their friendliness, between the military personnel and the civilians. It was a sort of propaganda film. Then they showed you the main picture."

—*Robert Chong, student*

Left: The most popular form of social entertainment was the movie. The cinema or gekizyo *was an agent of war propaganda.*

Above (left and right): In screening Japanese films such as The Great Sea Battles of Hawaii and Malaya *and* On to Singapore, *the Japanese were consciously dramatising the power of Japan.*

Above (left and right): Besides war movies, romantic films such as China Nite, *starring Lee Hsiang Lan, a popular actress and singer, proved to be a hit among the people.*

依靠英國
全本無歸

東亞的英國勢力完全隆落

行商貨英

舖店日親

貨日

此次
依靠日本
生意大吉

MAKE FORTUNE
BY COOPERATING
WITH JAPAN

Top: *On the economic front, anti-British propaganda leaflets were distributed.
To attain economic self-sufficiency, local people were encouraged to buy Japanese goods
and to conduct business with Japan.*

Bottom: *The teaching of Japanese language or* Nippon-go *was by far the most
important instrument to Nipponise the masses.*

Top and bottom: Numerous Japanese language schools were opened. The best-known among them was the Syonan Nippon Gakuen *(Syonan Japanese College) in Queen Street, which was set up by the* Gunseikanbu.

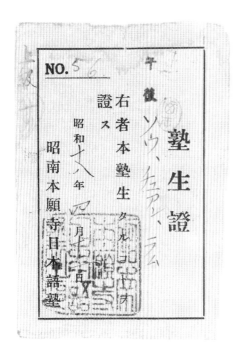

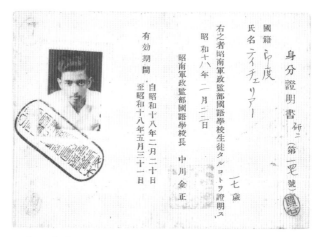

Left and above: Students of the Japanese language schools were issued with student identification cards.

Below (left): Badges of the various Japanese language schools in Singapore.

Below (right): Nippon-go *publications were the most effective learning tools. This* Nippon-go *textbook used by students at the* Syonan Nippon Gakuen *was written by its principal, Professor Kotaro Jimbo.*

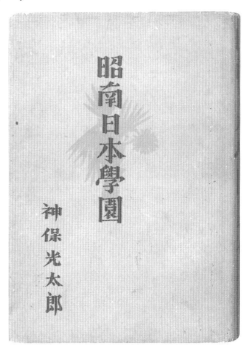

Right: The initial shortage of Nippon-go language books was overcome when more books were published.

Below: The deliberate policy of the Gunseikanbu to popularise Nippon-go motivated many working adults who realised the economic benefits to enrol in evening language classes.

LEARNING *NIPPON-GO*

"I think most of the students could take part in an ordinary conversation without much difficulty and could understand a Japanese who asked simple questions like: 'Where do you live?' or 'How long have you been staying in this place?'

"At first, we started with *katakana*. Then from *katakana*, we did *hiragana* which included *kanji*. At the beginners' course, we started mostly with *katakana* and then towards the end of the term we switched to *hiragana*. I had difficulty with *kanji*, which is Chinese characters, since I was English-educated. I had to practise a lot to be able to write *kanji* properly.

"Our principal suggested starting an Old Students' Union. He said we could get guest speakers and we could have study groups by ourselves and that way we could improve our knowledge of Japanese. We had regular meetings every week and we invited guest speakers with the help of other teachers.

"Occasionally, they got some of us to take part in singing lessons and to attend singing lessons. They even arranged for us to go to Alexandra Hospital to sing for the Japanese soldiers who were injured or who were sick.

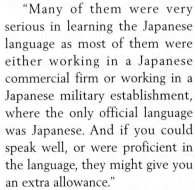

"Many of them were very serious in learning the Japanese language as most of them were either working in a Japanese commercial firm or working in a Japanese military establishment, where the only official language was Japanese. And if you could speak well, or were proficient in the language, they might give you an extra allowance."

—*Soh Chuan Lam, student of Japanese language*

Left (top and bottom): Students of Japanese language courses were required to sit tests before they could be promoted from the elementary, intermediate and advanced stages to attain the level of "research" class. Graduation ceremonies were often held to honour successful students.
Below: Teachers and students of the Syonan Nippon Gakuen *in Queen Street, 1943.*

SINGING JAPANESE SONGS

"Most of the songs were played in the morning during school assemblies … especially the national anthem [*Kimigayo*]. Singing was one of the programmes every day. It was one of the subjects. Every morning we have to sing the national anthem, then we march to the class. And before we go back every day, we would assemble in the school hall for some lectures and singing."

—*Victor Tan, student of Japanese language*

Left: A research class of the Syonan Nippon Gakuen, *1944.*

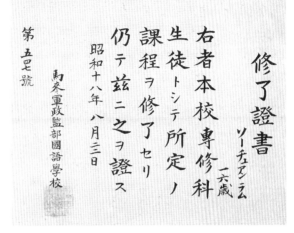

Left and above: Students who passed each stage were awarded certificates. These were awarded by the Syonan Honganji, *a private school at Oxley Rise, in 1942, and the* Malai Gunseikanbu Kakugo Gakko *(formerly* Syonan Nippon Gakuen*), in 1943.*

Above: Apart from raising the $50 million "gift" for the Japanese Military Administration, the Overseas Chinese Association was required to conduct Japanese language classes. This is an OCA language certificate issued in 1942.

Left: A certificate for graduating from the research class issued by the Syonan Honganji *in 1943.*

Above: The Syonan Tokubetsu Si Shihan Gakko, *a school set up in October 1943, had the dual function of training new* Nippon-go *teachers and retraining experienced ones.*
Below: A Nippon-go *examination paper set in the* Syonan Sinbun *for teachers.*

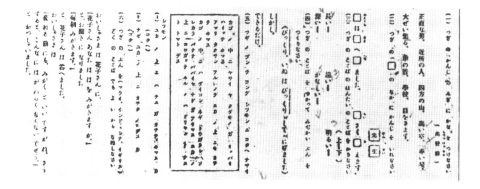

Right: To complement Nippon-go instruction in schools, the Syonan Broadcasting Station inaugurated its "Radio Nippon-go Lesson" on April 15, 1942. The programme was aired for ten minutes every evening. Listeners of the radio programme could refer to the Syonan Times or Syonan Sinbun for the contents of the lessons as they tuned in. They were simple and easy to follow.

...ing to give ...agle many anxious moments. This is the first time that this pair of scrappers have been matched in Syonan. Mr. Ho Kok Kee is the promoter.

Supporting bouts include scraps between Ignacio Fernandez and Tara Singh, and Slogger Chiang and Clever Mackey. Fernandez has proved in his recent fights that he is still a force to contend with while Slogger Chiang's apparently unorthodox style has turned out to be a difficult problem for many of his previous opponents.

The preliminaries include a bout between M. S. Voo and Rahman, and a curtain raiser. The card has been arranged as a slug-feast and much excitement is expected on Saturday.

ON THE AIR

TODAY'S PROGRAM

6 p.m. music; 6.20 p.m. Nippon language news for beginners; 6.30 p.m. Chinese Children's program; 6.50 p.m. religious talk; 7.20 p.m. news in Malai; 7.35 p.m. Mandarin choral songs; 8 p.m. news in Cantonese; 8.15 p.m. news in Hokkien; 8.30 p.m. Nippon Spirit through Her History, No. 8, in Malai; 8.40 p.m. Nippon language lesson; 8.55 p.m. Tamil religious songs; 9.20 p.m. news in Tamil; 9.35 p.m. news in Hindustani; 9.50 p.m. news in Nippon language; 10 p.m. news in English; 10.15 p.m. official bulletins; next day's program summary in ...

SYONAN SINBUN
NIPPON-GO LESSONS

LESSON 22
VOCABULARY

ヘ ン ジ	henji	answer	オーキイ	okii	big
ヨーフク	yofuku	clothes	ア ラ イ	arai	coarse
ト	to	door	ト ー イ	toi	far
ア メ	ame	rain	チ カ イ	chikai	near
ニ ジ	niji	rainbow	ウ マ イ	umai	tasty
クルマ	kuruma	rickshaw; car	マ ヅ イ	mazui	tasteless

EXERCISE

Nani o shite imashita ka? ナニ オ シテ イマシタ カ			What were you doing?
Henji o matte imashita ヘンジ オ マツテ イマシタ			I was waiting for a reply.
To o akete imashita ト オ アケテ イマシタ			I was opening the door.
Yofuku o tatande imashita ヨーフク オ タタンデ イマシタ			I was folding the clothes.
Heya o haite imashita ヘヤ オ ハイテ イマシタ			I was sweeping the room.
Kuruma o hiite imashita クルマ オ ヒイテ イマシタ			I was pulling the rickshaw.

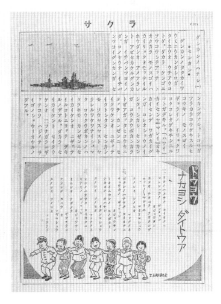

Left and below: The authorities promoted the acculturation of the local people by making Japanese customs and culture a part of their daily routine. An example of this was the Sakura Sinbun, a newsletter published by the Gunseikanbu for schoolchildren.

Left: To promote the idea of strict discipline among students and employees, the Japanese enforced the practice of bowing to the northeast, in the direction of the Japanese Imperial Palace in Tokyo, to pay respects to the Japanese Emperor.

Right and below (left and right): Apart from celebrating Japanese festivals like the New Year, the Japanese Emperor's birthday or Tenchyo Setsu was observed in various ways – from a simple acknowledgement of the day to elaborate and colourful parades.

奉祝天長節

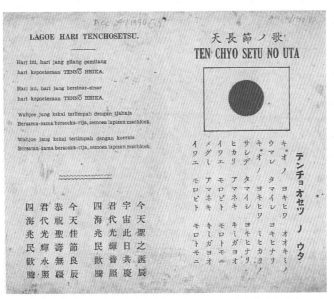

Above: Lyrics of a song to celebrate the Japanese Emperor's Birthday.
Below: Japanese concerts were also organised to foster the local population's appreciation of Japanese culture through music.

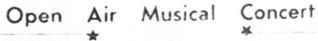

Part of the huge gathering that attended the first open air concert of Syonan's grand combined orchestra, at the former Y.M.C.A. ground in Bras Basah Road, under the baton of Conductor Makaoto Watanabe, in the Music for Everybody drive which has been proving so tremendously successful here

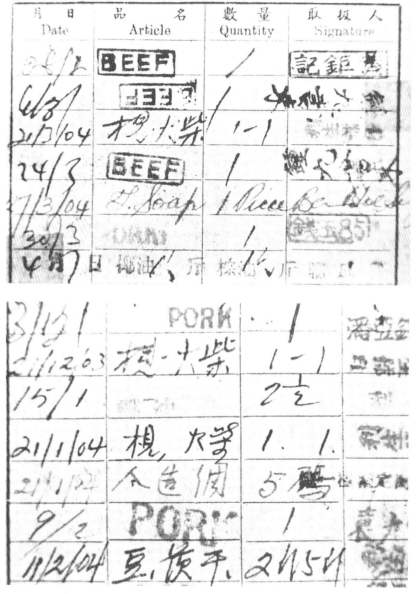

月 日 Date	品 名 Article	數 量 Quantity	取 扱 人 Signature
2 /2	BEEF	1	記錄 馬
6/3	BEEF	1	
2/3/04	椇 大柴	1-1	荣州
24/3	BEEF	1	
27/3/04	L. Soap 1 Rice		
30/3		1	錢 185
4月	日 燃油 斤 榛柴 斤		
3/12/	PORK	1	
2/12.03	椇 大柴	1-1	
15/1		2½	
21/1/04	椇 大柴	1. 1.	荣州
21/1/04	人造個	5	
9/2	PORK	1	
1/2/04	豆 庚平	2 1151	

Ration card.

Food Control

Food shortages were a salient feature of life during the Japanese Occupation. As pre-war Singapore had to import the majority of its food and consumer products, shortages occurred when its principal sources were cut off by the cessation of Singapore's entrepot trade.

As shortages caused food prices to soar, the local population turned to land cultivation for food. The Japanese policy to encourage self-sufficiency in food and other commodities caused much hardship to the people, whose efforts to grow their own food were only partially successful.

Besides growing their own food, those who could afford it turned to the black market to supplement their needs. The operation of the black market was often aided by the Japanese themselves. There was reportedly an influx of *rikenya* (concession-hunting profiteers), who used their connections with friends in the military to enrich themselves. The black-marketeers risked summary execution if caught and loss of capital without compensation. One serious consequence of black market activity was the spiralling cost of living for the local people.

The setting up of military-controlled syndicates like the *kumiai* did not help to improve the market conditions. In fact, these

THE SYONAN TIMES, WEDNESDAY, FEBRUARY 25, 2602, SYOWA 17   Page 3

NOTIFICATION
MARKET PRICES

Syonan, Feb. 25th, 2602.

ACCORDING to a notification of the Administration Office of Syonan Island the following order prohibits the upward trend of the price of commodities from what they were before the Great Oriental War. This order takes effect from Feb. 23, 2602.

Hereunder are indicated the maximum prices of various commodities to be observed in Syonan Island.

Anyone who purchases or sells any commodity above the prices hereunder indicated will be severely punished.

BY ORDER.

Above: Food prices were controlled by the Japanese Military Administration.

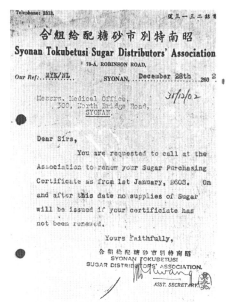

Left: To control the supply and ensure a fair distribution of essential foodstuffs such as rice, salt and sugar, appointed wholesalers and retailers were organised into various distributors' associations or kumiais.

syndicates monopolised the market and were believed to be responsible for causing the shortages. Instead of ensuring a fair distribution of food and other commodities, their priority was to meet the requirements of the military. Food supplies meant for public consumption were often siphoned off and found their way to the military units. Many people perished during the Japanese Occupation, either from malnutrition or disease.■

(4) Soya Beans will also be supplied to Rice Retailers, and they are hereby authorized to sell to those of their registered customers who may desire to buy same. One katty of Soya Beans per head per month. Purchase of Soya Beans, however, is not compulsory on the customers, and they are entitled to refuse buying same if they do not want to.

THE SYONAN-TO RICE & PADDY DISTRIBUTING ASSOCIATION.

November 14. 2602.

Right: The kumiais *would inform both retailers and consumers about the system of food distribution, and about any changes in the system.*

RICE DISTRIBUTION

"The government supply of food, rice and grains was put under the control of *kumiais*. In Singapore, I was told there were some 210,000 ration cards that relied on the distribution of rice by the government. One ration card was issued to at least two persons. On the average, some ration cards might even be for four or five persons.

"Supply of rice was distributed to the rice retailers. The rice and grain *kumiais* were able to control the warehouses and storage of grains. They would then instruct the rice distributors to issue to the rice retailers accordingly. It was stipulated that one *kati* [approximately 600 grams] should be sold at 10 cents. Even if you paid in Japanese currency, it was still 10 cents. That selling price remained stable right from the beginning. But the quality of rice was very poor."

—*Lim Soo Gan, rice merchant*

Left: The prices and quantity allowed of essential foods such as rice were fixed by the Food Control Department or Syokuhin-Ka, as indicated in this receipt.

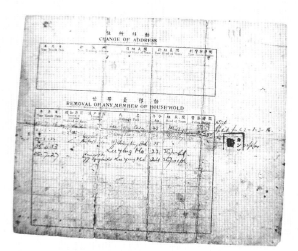

Above and right: Each family was given a ration card based on the number of household members recorded in the Peace Living Certificate and later in the Census Taking List which replaced it. The retailer's chop (stamp) on the back of the certificate or list ensured that consumers did not go elsewhere for another ration card.

SHORTAGE OF FOOD SUPPLIES

"We did not sell bread in our coffeeshop. Coffee beans, tea leaves and sugar were supplied by the Food Distributors' Association. We were given a licence to collect the commodities from the *kumiais*, but we had to pay for them. However, the rations given would not be enough. What could we do? When we ran out of coffee beans, we just closed shop. It had happened.

"I remembered we were open for business for about 20 days and then closed for the remaining days of the month. And I had to think of other means, like trading in the black market.

"During the early days of the Occupation, white sugar was still available. Later, when white sugar became increasingly scarce, we had to use coconut sugar as a substitute in making coffee.

"Initially, there were Malay and Indian food vendors who rented my stalls selling *nasi padang* and *roti prata*. They were forced to close when rice became unavailable. Our coffeeshop sold coffee and tea only and some soft drinks. In the earlier part of the Occupation, there were about one or two crates of soft drinks supplied to us. After that the soft drinks factory stopped production, we had no more soft drinks and beer to sell.

"Sugar was an expensive commodity then. When customers asked for extra sugar to be added in to their beverages, we could not oblige even when they were willing to pay for it. Sugar was very scarce then. At that time, it was unusual for a customer to ask for more sugar. Unlike nowadays, when we could hear customers saying: 'Not enough, could you please add more sugar.' During the Japanese Occupation days, we did not give customers extra sugar in their coffee or tea."

—*Teong Ah Chin, coffeeshop owner*

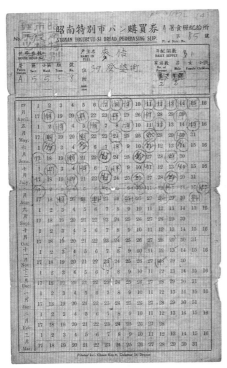

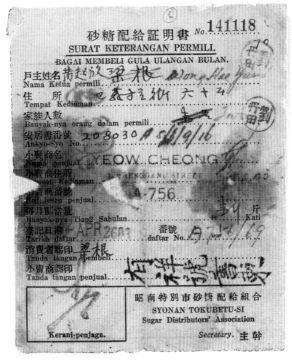

Above: Samples of various ration cards issued to consumers. Apart from the usual details including date, quantity and the licensed retailer's chop, the customer's particulars and those of his family members were given. All these ensured an organised system of rationing.

Right: A purchase permit for condensed milk. This special permit was only issued to households with sick members or infants under one year old.

Far right: When the rationing system began in March 1942, each person was allowed to buy 20 katis (about 12 kg) of rice per month. In 1943, the allowance was reduced to 14 katis (8¹/₂ kg). Just before the Japanese surrender in 1945, it was only 8 katis (5 kg) for a man, 6 katis (3¹/₂ kg) for a woman and 4 katis (2¹/₂ kg) for a child.

Below: A food distribution centre in Pulau Ubin.

RUBBER NOODLES

"Nowadays, our noodles are made of flour but during the Japanese Occupation, they were not. These noodles looked like plastic and were transparent when made. I do not know what type of flour they used. They were very tough, just like rubber.

"Nowadays, cooking oil is brushed on the noodles, whereas palm oil was used in the past. They were just like those red Chinese candles. The oil they used was red in colour, it had a kind of smell. Oh my, were they difficult to eat! But during the Japanese Occupation, we had no choice. We had to eat them even if they were not delicious. We had to use hot water to wash them. We had to wash them until there was no more of that oil, which resembled the melted wax of Chinese candles, before we cooked them.

"For the children, we just cooked some porridge that was more appetising. We adults just ate the rubber noodles and tapiocas. As for the men, they worked outside and so they were given rice and porridge to eat. We women just ate the rubber noodles and tapiocas, we just ate whatever we had."

—*Tan Ah Sang, housewife*

BLACK MARKET

"We asked them [the Japanese who worked in the stores] to deliver to a certain place. Normally we asked them to deliver to a kampong site, say, somewhere in Bukit Timah, Jurong or some remote places off town. Those were the safest places we could get. We could get the kampong people to help us by hiring their place for storage and we paid them.

"When the goods came, we needed to store for a day or two and then deliver to the customers. Any person caught would be beheaded. They have got informers around and if they come to know at which particular place and that a certain person was dealing illegal things from the army stores, they could come direct to that person. A few of my friends who were not careful enough were caught.

"The goods would be left there for a few days and we would be observing, to detect if anybody moves around that area. If [we received information] … that there was no one coming, then we would quickly transport the goods away."

—*Kenneth Chia, black market broker*

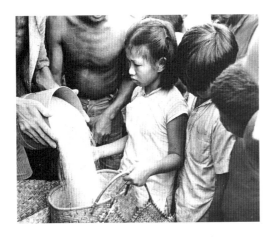

Above: Rations were inadequate for the average consumer and few could afford the black market prices for essential foodstuffs and commodities.

Left: On certain special occasions, such as the Japanese Emperor's Birthday, increased rations were distributed to eager hordes of people who would wait at the distribution centres throughout the night.

Left and below: In the latter half of the Occupation, as food shortages worsened, the local people were encouraged to become more self-sufficient by growing their own food. Even in the schools, vegetable gardens were cultivated by students and teachers. The photographs show students at St. Joseph's Institution, which was renamed Bras Basah School, hard at work on their small farm.

Below: Model farm schemes were initiated, and at this model farm in Geylang Serai, local people were encouraged to engage in farming. Guidance in farming techniques was also provided by the authorities.

THE SYONAN TIMES, FRIDAY, AUGUST 7, SYOWA 17

Grow More Food Campaign Should Not B Regarded As Somebody Else's Affair

GUNSEIBU OFFICIAL EMPHASIZES NEED FOR PUBLIC CO-OPERATION

RICE is the staple article of food for Malayans. All Malayans, Chinese and Indians, as a rule, eat rice daily. It must be noted, however, that the quantity of rice which the Malay Peninsula can produce is only 40 per cent. of the basic consumption needs of the country, while the remaining 60 per cent. has to be imported from Thailand or Burma, Mr. S. Yasuda of the Gunseibu, Syonan, pointed out in an interview with a representative of the Syonan Times.

Such conditions still go on unchanged in the days of the British Government. Among the products imported at first from other countries since our occupation of the Malay Peninsula was rice which still continues to be imported.

The British Government in Malaya preferred to have rice stored by residents to the building up of a reserve, if possible, at the cost of its own responsibility, leading the people to believe that there was an unlimited rice supply. Actually, the rice reserves throughout the Peninsula were very limited.

NEW FOOD POLICY EXPLAINED

To speed up self-sufficiency in staple foodstuffs within Malaya, the Nippon Military Administration has started a campaign to increase food production.

Explaining the purpose of the present drive, the Military Administration yesterday issued a special announcement on its new policy regarding staple foodstuffs.

The announcement emphasized on the attainment of self-sufficiency in foodstuffs involves the cultivation of all available land and the utilisation of idle farms production and distribution of agricultural implements and fertilizers, maintenance for fair prices for agricultural products...

Indians at work in a rice field in Malaya. Efforts are being made to increase rice production with a view to attaining self-sufficiency in this country.

To-Day's Radio Nippon-Go Lesson

IN your previous lesson learned the use of meaning "with" as preposition denoting the tools or instrument. To-day you will learn about other use of 'de' meaning "in English, denoting cause sometimes denotes exchange. Now here are some example.

1. Kare wa tyoki de kami nominasu — Hyoki—dedc—for; kuniei — medie nominasu—Like. Translation—He takes medicine for his illness.

2. Kaimu wake de kare Kimasen—Kanma wakufor this reason; kim des not come. Translation—He does not come for this reason.

3. Watashi wa kono katana en de ikimashita — shono ikimasita—bought shita for 10 en.

Above: To further boost production, a campaign encouraging people to grow more food was launched by the Japanese authorities.

Chinese Self-Sufficiency Pavilion

Above (left and right): Agricultural exhibitions were held to promote the idea of self-sufficiency. Such exhibitions usually lasted several weeks.

Right: Other exhibitions, such as the "Tropical Products Exhibition", encouraged the use of substitutes like tapioca, cornflour and coconut oil for making bread. Merit prizes were awarded for innovations.

WEDNESDAY, DECEMBER 15, KOKI 2603, SYOWA 18

Chinese To Participate In Self-Sufficiency Scheme Of

Ample Provisions To Be Made For Pioneer Settlers

AMENITIES INCLUDE SCHOOLS, PUBLIC HALLS, HOSPITAL, Etc.

BY OUR SPECIAL CORRESPONDENT

A FREE allotment of four acres of extremely fertile soil, free transport for personnel and essential requirements, supplies of rice, sugar and salt, and small monthly cash payments for the purchase of subsidiary foods for the first six months, and, above all, the oppor-

Left: As an indication of how seriously they viewed the problem of food supply, the Japanese authorities went so far as to sponsor the formation of agricultural settlements outside Singapore. The most prominent ones were the settlements at Endau and Bahau.

*Settlers clearing the land
for crop planting.*

New Settlements – Endau and Bahau

In August 1943, a mass evacuation from Singapore was ordered as a precaution against the possibility of the island becoming a war front again. The move, according to the Japanese, was also to ease the worsening food shortage situation.

People were encouraged to settle outside Singapore. The settlements were intended to be agricultural, and self-sufficient in rice and other produce. The settlement plan was made known to the public through the newspapers, and people responded to the plan as volunteers. To many, it was a major decision because it meant giving up work and moving away from relatives. However, it was a risk that some were prepared to take in exchange for a new lease of life and the promise of food. At least there was hope.

Community organisations and their leaders were approached by Mamoru Shinozaki from Syonan Municipality to work out some plans. The Overseas Chinese Association (OCA) showed enthusiasm in taking part, after being assured by Shinozaki that the military authorities would not interfere in the settlement project. A working committee was set up by the OCA and subcommittees were also formed to oversee various work requirements. Very quickly, funds were gathered and employees were recruited to implement the plan.

After the location in Endau, Johore, was identified, Shinozaki and committee members of the OCA visited the site. Temporary huts were constructed to house the settlers during the interim period before they were allocated land. As promised, Shinozaki

Above: Ching Kee Sun, chairman of the New Syonan Model Farm Construction Committee at Endau.

Right: An investigation team was selected to choose the site at Endau for the model farm. The task at hand was to clear the jungle, mark out roads, provide transportation and allocate plots to settlers.

kept the military authorities away and provided the daily necessities of the new settlers in the initial stages of the project.

The financing and management experience of the OCA leaders was considerable, and the Endau settlement, also known as New Syonan Model Farm, developed rapidly. Owing to the background of the Chinese settlers, some of whom had farming experience, many adjusted better in Endau compared to their counterparts who settled in Bahau.

The Eurasian Welfare Association and the Catholic Church were to be responsible for the Eurasians and other Catholics who were in favour of making a new home outside Singapore. However, the location chosen for the settlement – Bahau in Negri Sembilan – was not ideal and this group was also not as prepared financially as the Chinese community.

This settlement, commonly known as Fuji Village or *Fuji-go*, turned out to be less successful and was a bad experience for all. Many settlers in Bahau could not get used to farming and were infected by diseases. Shinozaki tried to meet the health needs of the settlers by providing medical supplies, but there was still a general shortage of medicine.

Towards the middle of 1945, locations in Batam and Bintang, Indonesian islands south of Singapore, were also identified as new settlements. But these were much smaller in scale than Endau and Bahau.■

Below: A letter of appointment to the health section of the Model Farm Committee, dated December 3, 1943. People were recruited into the various sections to assist the main committee in its work.

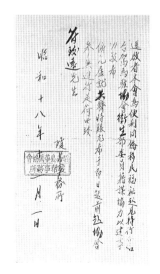

Far right: A receipt for a donation of $4,000 for the New Syonan Model Farm. The OCA raised $1 million to develop the farm.

Right: A letter for a resident of New Syonan. The settlement boasted a few major streets, shops, restaurants and a school.

Below left: By September 1944, about 12,000 people from Singapore had settled in New Syonan.

Below right: New Syonan developed well, due to the strong support of the OCA. Its food production was adequate and health record good.

SETTLING IN ENDAU

"I wanted a piece of land. I did not want to live from day to day in fear of making a mistake and being called away one of these days. So all these factors made me decide to go. And the promise of supply of rice. It was 7 or 8 *katis* [4 or 5 kg] per adult and half that for a child. And the most important thing was that we learnt finally that Endau was going to be solely in the charge of the Chinese Association, and the Japanese authorities were not allowed to interfere. That means the *Kempeitai* would be kept away.

"When we first arrived, we all had to live in those long huts first before we were allocated our lands. They distributed the lands to us later at the administrative office and had us sign the proper papers. There was a main road, and branching from the main road would be side roads which were named *lorongs*.

"As each batch of settlers came up to Endau, they would take the longhouse. That means they would have to prepare enough accommodation for the next batch to come along before they would bring them up. It takes a lot of preparation. They planned the thing very carefully. There would have to be drainage, sanitary conditions and a certain amount of privacy and cooking facilities. The minimal basic living conditions must be provided."

—*Gay Wan Guay, Endau settler*

Right: The Bahau settlement, Fuji Village, was established for the Eurasians and Chinese Roman Catholics under the leadership of Bishop Devals.

Left: The first batch of Bahau settlers left Singapore on December 28, 1943.

Below: A view of the main road running through Fuji Village. A community hut (left) was built for occasional gatherings, and opposite this was a police station.

Right: A typical hut in Fuji Village. This belonged to Dr J.B. van Cuylenburg, vice-president of the Eurasian Welfare Association. Few settlers built their own huts; many paid contractors to do the work.

DEATHS IN BAHAU

"It was a serious problem indeed. I don't think a day passed without somebody being brought to the mortuary. Deaths brought about by malaria. Whole families wiped out. They'd get malaria, they'd be so incapacitated, so weak, unable to help themselves. Their neighbours likewise – weak, unable to help themselves, unable to help their neighbours.

"Of course there were people who would go and provide some meals for them, but that's not enough. We needed medicines. We would feel the effects of the malaria, so enervating that it really knocked you out completely. We would be pale because it attacks your blood. We would have a feeling of fullness on the left side of our abdomen, indicating a very large spleen, tired easily. And trying to cultivate under these conditions was rather difficult.

"Malaria was brought about by mosquitoes. They had a sort of a team of oilers who would go and try and control malaria. But that was all done in vain. It was a vicious circle. Malaria would produce weakness, lower resistance. To combat that, you needed good food, nourishment which was not available. And after a while, the body just cannot take it any more. The body packs up and the patient dies."

—*Dr F.A.C. Oehlers, Bahau settler*

Right: Many settlers in Bahau had little knowledge of farming and therefore found living conditions hard. Moreover, the soil was poor and the site unhealthy. Malaria claimed many lives.

A typical street scene during the Japanese Occupation.

Daily Life under Japanese Rule

Above: People in Singapore had to keep track of changes in Japanese policies which affected them.

Although there was no more fighting on Singapore soil, the Japanese conquest did not bring the better life promised in pre-war Japanese propaganda. People in Singapore experienced severe control throughout the Occupation period. Almost every adult was required to carry or keep numerous documents at all times, including work pass, work badge, armband, ration card and daily necessities issued at work, allotment tickets for food, vehicle pass and radio pass. These measures were vital to Japanese efforts to maintain control, but were also the cause of much resentment.

Despite their fear and hatred of the Japanese, many people accepted jobs in the Japanese military units (*butai*) or Japanese businesses (*kaisha*). Some were employed as local civilian personnel such as police and clerical staff. Pre-war local businessmen generally kept a low profile; some of their businesses were seized by the military and they themselves worked for the Japanese. The internal conflict was great, especially for the Chinese, as they had always viewed Japan as an enemy. But the desire for survival and responsibility for their family made many swallow outraged dignity and patriotic feelings. It was a time for tenacity and sufferance.

As occupied territory, Singapore lost her free port status and her economy stagnated. The value of the currency issued by the

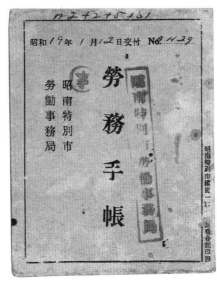

Far left: Occupied Singapore lost her free port status. Her economy stagnated and jobs were scarce. All men, whether employed or not, were called to register with the Malai Sumatra Komukanrikyokai (Labour Association), which was later replaced by the Syonan Municipality Labour Office.
Left: Labour booklets such as this were issued to employees.

Japanese, locally known as banana notes, dropped drastically as the war progressed. The British got hold of some local currency notes and printed tonnes of them at their base in India, and dropped them over Malaya to further sabotage the Japanese war economy.

To secure Japan's rule in the occupied territories, the Japanese civil administrators endeavoured to overcome problems such as shortages of food, daily necessities and medicines, along with unemployment and spiralling inflation. Merchants were encouraged to ship rice and other food from neighbouring areas in civilian vessels, to avoid Allied attacks. Black market activities were closely watched, in an effort to keep prices low and affordable. In general, the Japanese endeavoured to keep the livelihood of the people as normal as possible.

It was politically necessary to convince the Japanese back home of the stability of Japan's rule abroad. To create a picture of peace and prosperity in the occupied lands, pastimes such as sports were encouraged and supported by the administration.■

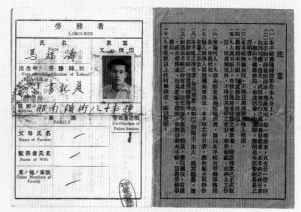

WORKING IN JAPANESE *BUTAI*

"When I finished my training in *Syonan Jidosha* [Vehicles] I was attached to *Butai 1516* at Bukit Timah 4th mile, the former University of Singapore. The one in charge of this workshop was a Staff Sergeant Hamaji San.

"Before we start work, every morning we have to do *taiso*, they called it, exercise. My brother was a foreman there, he had to stand in front of all of us in a group. He had to say the word in Japanese and we had to do the exercise. And after the exercise, then we do our normal duty, whatever jobs are given to us – repair brakes, recarbonising engines.

"My pay was $63 Japanese currency a month. We were given 16 cigarette coupons, if you want to buy cigarette from the canteen, you have to tear one, just like a stamp. Of course, the cigarette is not good. I admit that I did black market. My pay is only $63. If I go to Singapore town, a coffee will cost me $2 per cup. So before I go down [town], I will buy 40 cents of cigarette with my coupon which I sell black market – one packet is $60. Of course, I am very scared to sell them and very frightened, because once you get caught by the MP [Military Police], you're going to get it. So I usually go to the cigarette vendor at the corner and I used to make a sign of four with my fingers, then he knows I am going to give him four packets. So he gets ready the money, as soon as I got the money, I moved away."

—*Patrick Hardie, technician, Butai 1516*

Left: A work pass issued by Oka 1615 Butai (military unit) in April 1943. The Japanese military authorities became the main employer during the Occupation. Many locals had to work for them to survive.

*Left (top and bottom):
Certain essential
businesses and
industries were in the
hands of the butais.
This attendance book
belonged to a worker
of Oka 15813 Butai,
which manufactured
ammunition at River
Valley Road. On one
side of the book is the
worker's number; the
other side indicates
his work station, race,
name and age. The
page inside records his
attendance in January
and February 1944.*

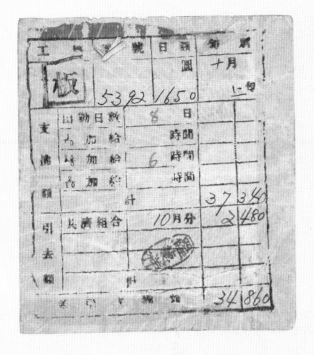

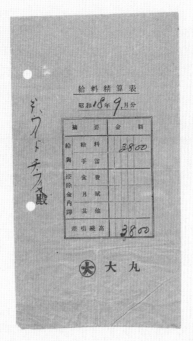

FAMILIES UNITE TO SURVIVE

"I think family became closer because of the danger and all that. Everybody had to depend on each other. Having a big family and having so many mouths to feed, I think our problem was how to get the funds in order to feed them. In fact, almost every one of us who was able to work just worked – for instance, the ladies, what they do? Those who can, they go and work for a chap who is sewing dresses for the navy. So whoever can sew would just join that firm and earn something.

"At that time the important thing is not only earning the money, it is when you go there, you get rations. Those who are not working, they will go into estates and collect dry wood for firewood. My daughter who was just only 6 or 7 years old, she was carrying tea to supply to the Japanese officers in the factory. So everyone does something for the family."

—*Tan Guan Chuan, civilian*

Above left: A pay slip from Oka 15813 Butai for the first half of October. The worker was also paid for overtime work.

Left and above right: Work badge of Sogo, a Japanese store, and pay slip dated September 1943. The Japanese military authorities encouraged the Japanese to set up businesses in occupied lands. Such businesses were often used for propaganda in Japan to show the strength of the Japanese Empire.

Top left: Ration record book. People worked not so much for the wages, as they could never hope to catch up with the spiralling living costs. They worked for the rations given by butais *(military units). Employees received cigarettes, rice and beans rations periodically.*
Top right: Other fringe benefits included allotment tickets for salted fish and tapioca flour.
Bottom: Local people were allowed to carry on their small businesses. Japanese business signs were displayed.

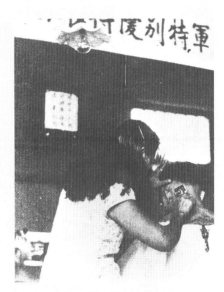

Right: Some businesses, like this barber shop, offered discounts to Japanese soldiers. The soldiers were known for taking things from shops without paying until they were stopped by the Japanese Military Police.

JAPANESE-APPOINTED PHOTO STUDIO

"Introduced by my friend, I went to apply for a military-appointed licence. Once I had this licence, a lot of Japanese came to take photographs and I was also asked to go to army camps to take photographs.

"All photographs taken must be submitted to YMCA [*Kempeitai*] for inspection. I must go there every day. Supposing the photographs were ready in the morning, I would bring them there for stamping and then bring them back for customers' collection. They inspected every photograph. Before I got the military-appointed licence, when the Japanese came, they shouted and beat you first, and then said, 'Take photograph!' Later when my photo studio became the military-appointed studio and I hung up the sign, every Japanese who came in was very polite, they would bow and say, '*konichiwa*' before coming in."

—*Lim Ming Joon, proprietor, Daguerre Photo Studio*

Far left: Certain shops, known as "military-appointed" shops, were shortlisted by the military to cater for the Japanese. This is an advertisement for a military-appointed restaurant.

Left: Japanese political vocabulary was adopted by local businesses. In this case the name "Great East Asia" was given to a restaurant.

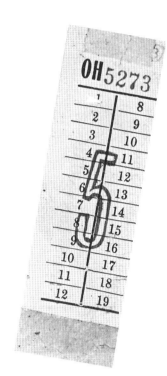

自轉車登錄證
BICYCLE REGISTRATION CARD.

許可証發行番號
Identity Card No. 59772

自轉車番號
Bicycle No. 昭 59772

所有者
Issued to *Leo Kah Tong*

住所
Address *139, Koon Seng Road*

發行日
Date *1/9/42*

Above: Bicycle registration card. All bicycles had to be registered with the Registrar of Vehicles.

Above, top right and bottom right: The Japanese Military Administration permitted Japanese companies to run certain businesses previously owned by the British or Chinese. The Tokyo Express Transport and Tramway Company took control of almost all bus and car transportation in Malaya and Singapore. The tram-bus resumed its service in March 1942. Bus fare was printed on the ticket.

SYONANSI SIDEN.
2nd CLASS 5 CENTS.
NOT TRANSFERABLE.

SURVIVING WITH SUBSTITUTES

"Like they say, necessity is the mother of invention. We learnt to make soap. I remember we used to cook a big lot of coconut oil with something else and then we had soap. We used to buy the fresh milk and we put sugar and cooked it for hours till we had condensed milk, which could be kept, otherwise the milk would go bad.

"During the Japanese time, we were quite clever people. We knew how to make a lot of things. We made wine and tapioca crackers – a lot of essential stuff they made out of tapioca. That was the only stuff they could get to make cakes after we had no flour."

—*Mdm Chu Shuen Choo, housewife*

Above: A bus engine being fixed at the rear of the bus to enable it to run on charcoal. This wartime invention was born out of necessity as fuel was scarce.

Right: The Syonan Times *reported the invention of the trishaw, another form of transportation, by a Mr Sunny Tan of Balestier Road. It was to become very popular in later years.*

Right: Recreation outlets were few. Some people were able to afford an occasional outing to watch a movie. Such fun could, however, turn into a nightmare. The Japanese military authorities sometimes raided places like cinemas to round up youths for workgangs.

Left: Receipt and badge of the Syonan Sports Association. In order to keep up the appearance of stability in the occupied lands, the Japanese military authorities allowed the locals to organise sport activities.

Right: The Syonan Sports Association picked players from different soccer league teams to form the Singapore team. It once played against the German Navy team which was visiting Singapore. Participating in games helped to alleviate the tension caused by uncertainty under Japanese rule.

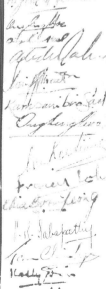

Right: Vaccination certificate issued in May 1942. The Japanese authorities were concerned about the spread of diseases. Despite the shortage of medicine, the Syonan Municipality issued an order in April 1942 for compulsory vaccination.

Below: Mobile clinics were sent out by the Syonan Municipality to visit the sick. However, malnutrition – like beri-beri, so common during wartime – was difficult to cure.

BERI-BERI

"At that time, most people suffered from beri-beri. I think generally because of lack of good food. And then if you want to get injection for beri-beri, you don't get. You want to get vitamin pills also you don't get – very expensive. I had beri-beri. Fortunately at that time I had a cousin who was working in the Japanese hospital. So I get Vitamin B1 injections and also pills. I remember the first time I suffered from that I was given ten injections. And then after that I recovered."

—*Tan Guan Chuan, civilian*

Right: Lottery tickets were sold to raise funds for Syonan Municipality projects. The proceeds from the Konan Saiken went towards relief funds for the needy as well as sanitary and health improvement schemes.

Far right: The Engo Saiken raised funds for the relief of war victims.

FEELINGS TOWARDS JAPANESE RULE

"The only hope of the Malays was that maybe under the Japanese, they will be better off than under the British. That was the reason why initially they were pro-Japanese. [The Japanese] were so brutal. They don't care whether you are Chinese, whether you are Malay. At road blocks, if you don't bow to them properly, or you can't answer their question, they will simply slap you. That's also some of the reasons why the Malays don't like them.

"The living conditions at that time were almost universal to all people, whether they are Malays, Chinese or Indians. They were all hard up. Not only they are hard up, they feared of this *Kempeitai*. They feared the Japanese brutality. Actually, we were not happy during the Japanese time. We can't get enough food, cannot get our clothing. If the Japanese had been here for another year, I think a lot of people would have died of starvation."

—*Ismail Zain, civilian*

Far left: A post office savings book. The Japanese authorities put great effort into promoting a savings campaign, but as most people were living from hand to mouth, the response was poor.

Left: Japanese banks also set up branches in Singapore, as shown by this bank advertisement.

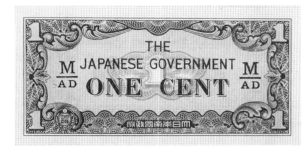

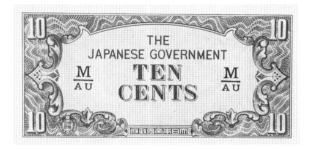

Above: The wartime Japanese economy could not support a prolonged war. Faced with runaway inflation, the Japanese administration merely printed more currency notes for circulation.

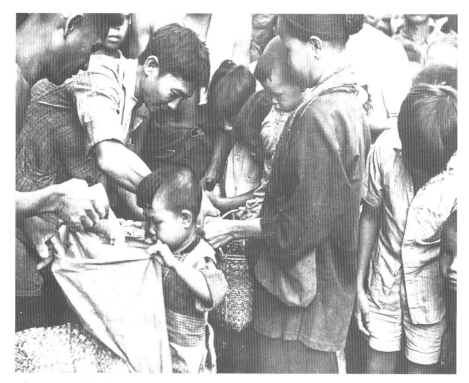

Above: Acute food and material shortages led to the formation of a black market. But even within the black market there was rocketing inflation. In December 1943, one kati *(600 grams) of rice cost $3.60 (Japanese currency). By August 1945, the price had risen to $108 per* kati.

Opposite: Black-marketeering was rampant. The Japanese took action against offenders but stamping out the illicit trade proved to be an impossible task.

Black Market Operators Fined $4,750

FOUR CHINESE,
stolen rice in the
were fined a total o
Syonan Keizi Tihoh
They were Lai Me
Lim, Kiang Boon S
Kim Thye.

Three of these ac
keepers, and the fourt
as the proprietor of a

Sold Stolen Rice In Black Market

Abetted Disposal Of Stolen Paper In Black Market

A CHINESE, Tang Wocn Yew,
who allegedly dealt in the black
market was sentenced to one
imprisonment
(in default, two
mprisonment) in
Tihohoin yes-

pleaded guilty to
ient of profiteering.

Fined $1,000 For Profiteering On Medicinal Tablets

FINES totalling $1,000, or one
year's rigorous imprisonment in
default, was imposed in the Syonan Keizi Tihohoin yesterday on
a Chinese, Leong Yap Pin, who
pleaded guilty to two counts of
profiteering on certain medicinal
tablets.

A hawker in Rochore Road, the
accused was stated to have sold, on
two occasions in May, a total of 50 of
these tablets above the fixed price of
three cents each.

WITHOUT A PERMIT

Pleading guilty to a charge of unlawful possession of arms, a Chinese,
Chua Jin Huat, was sentenced to a

ED in
n Satur
d three
t bags c
es. T
tolen fr
p, was s
m $80 tc
before Mi
Syonan
appeared
sentence
risonment
urther tw
r-
accused,
d to two
and a f
months'

w Ngung
hird and
tenced to
ment and
months'

Profiteered On Nails, Two Chinese Fined

FINES, totalling $1,100, were
imposed in the Syonan Keizi
Tihohcin on Tuesday on two Chinese, Teo Boon Kai and Wee
Choo Huat, after the men had
pleaded guilty to charges of profiteering and abetment of profiteering on nails.

The case was a sequel to a deal on
June 19 when the first accused was
stated to have bought 64 katis of nails
from one Soh Beng Cher, at the price
of $416, the second accused acting as
broker.

These nails formed part of a lot
alleged to have been stolen from a
government store in Wallich Street on
June 18, according to the prosecution
officer, who added that Police investi-
gations into the theft had led to
the arrest of the three men.

The judge fined Teo Bocn Kai, described as a carpenter residing in
Amoy Street, $750 or nine months'
rigorous imprisonment in default, and

Propaganda poster
showing Japanese victory.

Japanese Defence Build-up

The Japanese military, fully aware that they were engaged in a world war, worked out a defence strategy for each of the occupied territories. The longer the frontier, the more difficult it was to defend. The long Japanese supply lines were vulnerable to enemy attack, particularly when the Japanese naval and air forces were engaged at the frontier and unable to provide cover.

By mid-1942, four months into the Japanese Occupation, the people of Singapore were enrolled in regular air raid precaution exercises. This was followed by the implementation of lights control. The Fire Fighting Corps and Labour Service Corps were set up to assist the military in building up the defence.

The Japanese recruited local youths of all races into the military forces. They were auxiliary in nature but were given military training. Initially, they were assigned to do odd jobs in the camps. However, as the war situation turned against the Japanese in 1944, many local recruits were sent into active duty.

The reaction of the people towards the Japanese defence was mixed. On one hand, many silently and anxiously anticipated the defeat of the Japanese and the return of the British. On the other, they were worried about another wave of destruction which would be caused by an Allied counter-attack. Community leaders were caught in the conflict between fulfilling military requests by involving civilians in Japanese defence works, and the reluctance of the civilians themselves to take part.

The effectiveness of the locals in carrying out defence work was questionable. Many had viewed the Japanese as invaders

Above: Local people were drawn into the preparation for an Allied counter-attack. A defence poster design contest was organised by the Japanese authorities to promote awareness of the defence of Malaya.

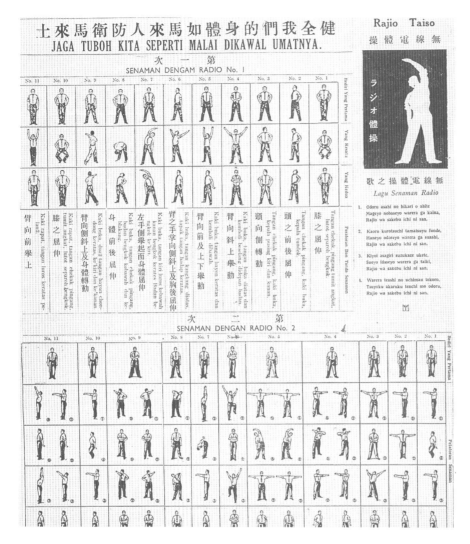

Left and opposite (top): A radio exercise programme was launched to encourage the locals to keep fit.

and cruel conquerors. Realistically, little could be expected from the locals by way of cooperation.

Burma was considered a major Japanese defence front. Consequently, a strong Japanese force was established there until January 1945, when the Americans launched an attack on the Philippines that threatened the Japanese mainland. When that happened, Japanese troops in Burma were left to fight the Burmese war without further reinforcements, while the Philippines became a strategic point in the Japanese defence. In comparison, Singapore and Malaya played a relatively small role in the Japanese military strategy. ■

Below and bottom left: In May 1943, the recruitment for Heiho (also known as Gunpo or auxiliary servicemen) was introduced. Teenagers recruited for basic training were provided with lodging and clothing. They served under the military, performing miscellaneous duties. Some were later sent with Japanese soldiers to pursue anti-Japanese resistance forces in the Malayan jungles.

Left: On December 8, 1943 the Giyu-gun (Voluntary Army) and Giyu-tai (Voluntary Corps) were introduced.

FIRE FIGHTING CORPS

"The Japanese put up a notice in *Syonan Jit Pau*. It said those who did not work for the military must take part in first-aid or fire-fighting. Everyone must go for the training. The three-star man [auxiliary police assistant] in my area made a house to house visit. He said, 'If you are not working for the government, you must take part in fire-fighting or first-aid.' So I took part in fire-fighting.

"My area was in Silat Road. I trained twice a week in the afternoon at about four or five o'clock. It [fire-fighting] was taught by a Japanese. He spoke in Japanese, we watched his gestures. We had to learn what it was called in Japanese. We were trained how to use the fire-fighting machine. We later went to fire brigade for formal training, it was conducted in English.

"We were all volunteers and did not get any pay. We waited until the siren was off, then we came out to the streets. Sandbags were placed at several places along the street. If the street was hit by bombs we extinguished the fire with sand. We could not use water to extinguish fire caused by incendiary bombs. If the street caught fire, we would do our work immediately. If the house caught fire, we could not do anything."

—*Lee Chui Tong, member of the Fire Fighting Corps*

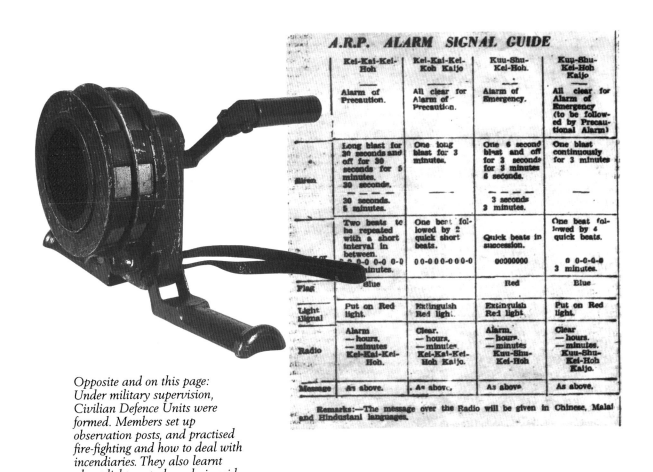

A.R.P. ALARM SIGNAL GUIDE

	Kei-Kai-Kei-Hoh.	Kei-Kai-Kei-Koh Kaijo	Kuu-Shu-Kei-Hoh.	Kuu-Shu-Kei-Hoh Kaijo
	Alarm of Precaution.	All clear for Alarm of Precaution.	Alarm of Emergency.	All clear for Alarm of Emergency (to be followed by Precautional Alarm)
Siren	Long blast for 30 seconds and off for 30 seconds for 5 minutes. 30 seconds. 30 seconds. 5 minutes.	One long blast for 3 minutes.	One 6 second blast and off for 3 seconds for 3 minutes 6 seconds. 3 seconds 3 minutes.	One blast continuously for 3 minutes
	Two beats to be repeated with a short interval in between. 0 0 0-0 0-0 0-0 minutes.	One beat followed by 2 quick short beats. 00-000-000-0	Quick beats in succession. 00000000	One beat followed by 4 quick beats. 0 0-0-0-0 3 minutes.
Flag	Blue		Red	Blue
Light signal	Put on Red light.	Extinguish Red light.	Extinguish Red light	Put on Red light.
Radio	Alarm. — hours. — minutes Kei-Kai-Kei-Hoh.	Clear. — hours. — minutes Kei-Kai-Kei-Hoh Kaijo.	Alarm. — hours. — minutes Kuu-Shu-Kei-Hoh	Clear. — hours. — minutes Kuu-Shu-Kei-Hoh Kaijo.
Message	As above.	As above.	As above	As above.

Remarks:—The message over the Radio will be given in Chinese, Malai and Hindustani languages.

Opposite and on this page: Under military supervision, Civilian Defence Units were formed. Members set up observation posts, and practised fire-fighting and how to deal with incendiaries. They also learnt about light controls and air raid precautions and how to operate sirens like the one above.

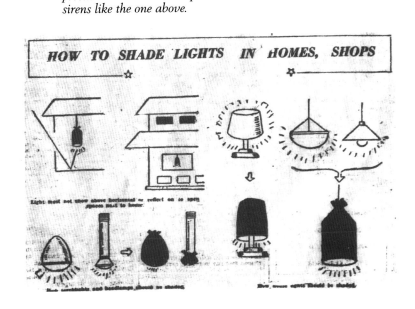

HOW TO SHADE LIGHTS IN HOMES, SHOPS

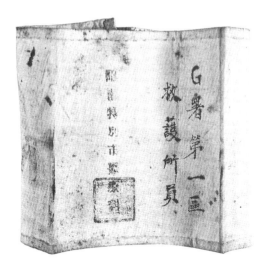

Left: First-aid posts were set up. Armbands of this type were issued to first-aid members.

Left and above: Armband and badge of the Blue Cross. With the approval of the Syonan Municipality, a charitable organisation, the Blue Cross, was formed by five Chinese worshipping halls in 1943. It operated free feeding centres, removed dead bodies and looked after the victims during Allied bombings.

Right: Employees of the Japanese Military Administration had to join the Special Forward Corps. In emergencies, male members did field duty while female members remained at their posts attending to casualties. A special identity card printed with the motto was issued.

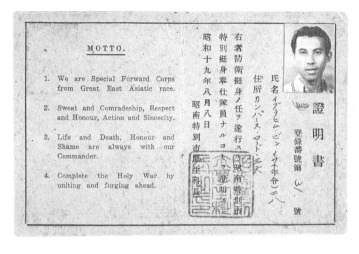

MOTTO.

1. We are Special Forward Corps from Great East Asiatic race.

2. Sweat and Comradeship, Respect and Honour, Action and Sincerity.

3. Life and Death, Honour and Shame are always with our Commander.

4. Complete the Holy War by uniting and forging ahead.

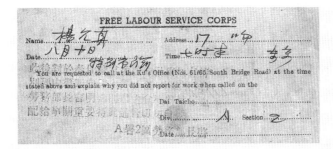

Left and below: As the war progressed, labour was needed for defence work such as digging trenches, carrying ammunition, packing army stores, and for farms owned by the butais (military units). This work notice and armband were for men enlisted by the Free Labour Service Corps.

LABOUR SERVICE CORPS

"I remember that I have to go. I being the leader, and my colleagues about 30 of them, compulsory, asked to go to do Labour Corps job with the Japanese military at Ama Keng, right inside a rubber plantation. I managed to meet a Japanese officer, he explained that we were there purely on a voluntary basis to help to dig trenches. So early in the morning, we got up to assemble, to collect all the equipment for digging the trenches. We worked there for a week. You don't get paid for it. They don't give you anything like rice ration. What you get was your daily supply for one week digging trenches.

"All the time, we all look forward to the last day to come. On the eve of departure, a few military trucks came in. They were loaded with civilians. They were all males, able-bodied men. I was called up by one Japanese in the middle of the night. I was a bit astonished why they came at such late night. Then one of them spoke to me: 'We were called up or pulled up on the streets in town after a cinema show or just walking along.' The Japanese asked me to interpret to them, 'You all got to work for a few days, have no fear. You will dig trenches. You all will be given food, everything.' Where they slept, where they were put to stay, I can't remember, because the next morning we left. Home sweet home."

—*Robert Chong, employee of* Noda Shoyu Kaisha

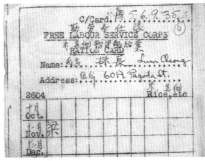

Far left: Labour exemption notice. Every group of 150 men had to supply 20 workers aged from 15 to 45. Some, however, including employees of the Overseas Chinese Association (OCA), were exempted.
Left: Labourers were not paid wages, but received rice, sugar or cigarettes at the end of the day.

Malayan People's Anti-Japanese Army (MPAJA).

CHAPTER THIRTEEN

Anti-Japanese Resistance

T he growth of local resistance can be traced to pre-Occupation military arrangements made by the British. In May 1941, the British established the headquarters of Oriental Mission in Singapore to plan and operate subversive activities in enemy-controlled lands.

After the Japanese landing at Kota Bharu, some European planters, miners and civil servants, and Chinese communists whom the British felt could be useful in military action, were recruited and trained at 101 Special Training School, situated in Singapore. These people, known as the "left-behind parties", were later sent in batches to locations where weapons and explosives were hidden for use when the invaders arrived. By the end of January 1942, about 163 men were in position; the Chinese communists were allocated areas where Communist Party membership was strong. John Davis of the Malayan Police Force and Richard Broome, a senior civil servant, were involved in this operation and managed to escape when Singapore fell to the Japanese.

Just before the fall of Singapore, the communist members were advised to move into the jungle. From their jungle camps, they took every opportunity to harass the Japanese as they awaited the return of the British. Survivors of the European "left-behind parties" were later found together with the communists. By 1943, the resistance movement, led by the communists, had grown significantly and was known as the Malayan People's Anti-

Above: From their base in India, the British wasted no time in implementing their counter-attack plans. A group of officers who had served in pre-war Malaya were to be sent back for sabotage work and to contact those who had been planted there by the British just before the fall of Singapore. Richard Broome (left) and John Davis (second from left) were two leaders of this mission, known as Force 136 (Malaya Section).

Without Chinese assistance, the secret mission to Malaya was impossible. The officer-in-charge, Basil Goodfellow (right), persuaded Lim Bo Seng (left), whom he met on board a ship while evacuating from Singapore, to join the mission.

Japanese Army (MPAJA). Members of the movement continued to receive training from some Europeans who had stayed behind.

Back in India and Ceylon (Sri Lanka), the British formed the Force 136 Mission to organise sabotage activities all over Malaya, behind enemy lines. Agents were recruited and trained for this purpose. Force 136 launched "Operation Gustavus I" in May 1943, a series of submarine sorties to the Perak coast of Malaya led by John Davis. The objectives were to send the agents back to establish links, to create an intelligence system, to contact the resistance forces and to look for survivors of the "left-behind parties". Force 136 reached an agreement with MPAJA. Unfortunately, Force 136 suffered heavy losses when their agents were arrested in March 1944. They did not resume communications with India until February 1945.

In October 1944, Force 136 launched "Operation Carpenter" from Australia, led by W.B. Martin, to infiltrate South Johore. They established communications with their headquarters on October 15, 1944 and were able to transmit useful information on the movements of Japanese warships in and out of Singapore. They also established contact with the 4th Regiment of MPAJA.

In order to organise a Malay resistance movement, Force 136 sent "Operation Hebrides" in December 1944. They made a blind drop from an air force Liberator in North Perak. Malay agents were recruited and used for intelligence work. Subsequently, Operations "Fighter", "Beacon" and "Multiple" were sent into Kedah and Pahang.

Right: These recruits received special intelligence training at Poona, India. The "folboat" was used for secret landing.

The British were aware of the communist influence in MPAJA, but they also knew that MPAJA was the most important resistance group in Malaya. As far as the British were concerned, as long as the communists confined themselves to purely military concerns, they were prepared to arm them. The British expected them to play a significant role in attaining an Allied victory when the counter-attack of Malaya finally took place.■

Above: Through Lim Bo Seng, Chinese agents were recruited from China and from among the Malayan Chinese who had evacuated to India.

Top: *The first party of Force 136, led by John Davis, landed in May 1943 at Segari in Perak. This photograph was taken at the Force 136 headquarters at Mt Bidor in Perak in 1945.*

Bottom left: *Lim Bo Seng (code name Tan Choon Lim) landed in Malaya in November 1943 to supervise the Chinese agents. In March 1944, along with four other Chinese agents, he was arrested by the Japanese and died of dysentery in prison three months later.*

Bottom right: *Led by the Malayan Communist Party (MCP), the Malayan People's Anti-Japanese Army (MPAJA) used posters to attract people to join the guerilla movement. Its founding members were from the "left-behind parties", and had received basic military training from the British.*

CONTACTING THE ANTI-JAPANESE ARMY

"Davis sent me to Pangkor Island because many Teochews resided there. I opened a shop known as Chop Tien Seng. I obtained two licences, one for the wholesale of rice, the other for retailing. This was how I contacted the anti-Japanese army.

"Every shop must contribute $25 per month to the anti-Japanese army. The person who came to collect the money was Lim Hai. Davis told me if he was sent by Chin Peng, I should give him more money. That day, Lim Hai came, I could not tell him that the Allies wanted to contact the anti-Japanese forces. So I said, 'Mr Lim, I want to contribute more money and I want to meet Chin Peng.' There was an island known as San Poh Kong Lee Lao Koon Jen. Chin Peng met me there. When he saw me, he said, 'You are a running dog! You are a traitor! You intend to catch me?'

"I took them to the beach at Segari, where we buried our wireless and documents. These were my evidence – we were the Allies. He said, 'So we are compatriots.' That night, they threw a welcome party for me. I went to their base. I must go to the tiger den if I want to meet the tiger – nothing ventured, nothing gained. Chin Peng and I sat together, we were very happy."

—*Lee Han Kong, member of the first landing party, Force 136*

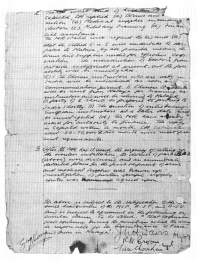

Left: It took Force 136 about three months to contact MPAJA after their first landing. In December 1943, a treaty was signed between the British and MPAJA. Members of MPAJA were to be given military training and supplies and would serve under Louis Mountbatten's Southeast Asia Command.

MPAJA vs THE JAPANESE

"They [the Japanese troops] were less likely to see us. First of all, we were a small group, secondly, we were all gathered in one place. Once we opened fire, we would flee. The enemy would not dare advance because they wanted to be sure before they stepped forward. By then we had already retreated to some distance.

"The most important thing to bear in mind was not to attack the vanguards. If we struck at the vanguards, we would give their main troops the opportunity to plan a strategy to attack us. So we let the vanguards come and go. Sure enough, after that the main troops would arrive. We have learnt from experience how to detect their presence; they made a lot of noise, chopped the trees, talked above their voices and sang. These were the vanguards who opened up roads, chopping off trees for troops' movement. This in a way was telling us that they [the Japanese main troops] would be coming.

"The Japanese had launched a massive attack on us. The last attack was about three or four months before the surrender. It was like guerilla tactics, one troop with about 100 to 200 men came, then retreated, another troop came, then retreated. Their intention was to make us on the run all the time and not able to rest. We had to be always on the move – stay at one place for two nights and then move on to another place for two nights. The Japanese plan was to wipe us out."

—*Chia Chore Seng, member of the 4th Independent Regiment, South Johore*

Above: More Force 136 groups were parachuted into Malaya after February 1945. The Allied attack plans were set and the resistance forces were ready.

Left: Flag of the MPAJA 1st Independent Regiment, based in Selangor. MPAJA had eight regiments with some 10,000 able fighting men based in major Malayan states.

Left and below: Compass watch and ear compass (smaller than the modern Singapore one-cent coin) used by MPAJA agents. MPAJA had a network in Singapore collecting military intelligence on the Japanese, as well as donations of money, food and medicine.

UNDERGROUND WORK

"I was given a leaflet and I showed it to people who were interested. I did not pass it around. I also gathered donations and the liaison person would come and collect from me. I remember one day, I was given some posters, they read: 'Down with the Japanese imperialist!' and 'Down with the traitor!'

"The leader asked us to go round pasting posters. We did not know how serious it was. When there were no Japanese soldiers around, we quickly pasted it up and then quickly ran away. The next day, many people went to see the poster. I dare not see it myself. I pasted posters mainly in Jalan Besar area. There were two of us doing this. At that time, I was brave. I was running around the streets at midnight. Later I was arrested. We were known as anti-Japanese unit. I was always contacted by the same person. She was a woman. She was also arrested and later hanged. She was young."

—*Mdm Chew Lee Ngor, member of the underground network*

Right: Once arrested, those involved in anti-Japanese underground work were either executed or sentenced to life imprisonment in Outram Jail.

INSTRUMENT OF SURRENDER OF JAPANESE FORCES UNDER
THE COMMAND OR CONTROL OF THE SUPREME COMMANDER,
JAPANESE EXPEDITIONARY FORCES, SOUTHERN REGIONS,
WITHIN THE OPERATIONAL THEATRE OF THE SUPREME
ALLIED COMMANDER, SOUTH EAST ASIA.

1. In pursuance of and in compliance with :

    (a) the Instrument of Surrender signed by the Japanese plenipotentiaries by command and on behalf of the Emperor of Japan, the Japanese Government, and the Japanese Imperial General Headquarters at Tokyo on 2 September, 1945 ;

    (b) General Order No. 1, promulgated at the same place and on the same date ;

    (c) the Local Agreement made by the Supreme Commander, Japanese Expeditionary Forces, Southern Regions, with the Supreme Allied Commander, South East Asia at Rangoon on 27 August, 1945 ;

to all of which Instrument of Surrender, General Order and Local Agreement this present Instrument is complementary and which it in no way supersedes, the Supreme Commander, Japanese Expeditionary Forces, Southern Regions (Field Marshal Count Terauchi) does hereby surrender unconditionally to the Supreme Allied Commander, South East Asia (Admiral The Lord Louis Mountbatten) himself and all Japanese sea, ground, air and auxiliary forces under his command or control and within the operational theatre of the Supreme Allied Commander, South East Asia.

2. The Supreme Commander, Japanese Expeditionary Forces, Southern Regions, undertakes to ensure that all orders and instructions that may be issued from time to time by the Supreme Allied Commander, South East Asia, or by any of his subordinate Naval, Military or Air-Force Commanders of whatever rank acting in his name, are scrupulously and promptly obeyed by all Japanese sea, ground, air and auxiliary forces under the command or control of the Supreme Commander, Japanese Expeditionary Forces, Southern Regions, and within the operational theatre of the Supreme Allied Commander, South East Asia.

3. Any disobedience of, or delay or failure to comply with, orders or instructions issued by the Supreme Allied Commander, South East Asia, or issued on his behalf by any of his subordinate Naval, Military or Air Force Commanders of whatever rank, and any action which the Supreme Allied Commander, South East Asia, or his subordinate Commanders, acting on his behalf, may determine to be detrimental to the Allied Powers, will be dealt with as the Supreme Allied Commander, South East Asia may decide.

4. This Instrument takes effect from the time and date of signing.

5. This Instrument is drawn up in the English language, which is the only authentic version. In any case of doubt as to intention or meaning, the decision of the Supreme Allied Commander, South East Asia is final. It is the responsibility of the Supreme Commander, Japanese Expeditionary Forces, Southern Regions, to make such translation into Japanese as he may require.

Signed at Singapore at 0341 hours (G.M.T.) on 12 September, 1945.

陸軍大將寺内壽一

SUPREME COMMANDER
JAPANESE EXPEDITIONARY FORCES,
SOUTHERN REGIONS.

Louis Mountbatten

SUPREME ALLIED COMMANDER,
SOUTH EAST ASIA.

The Japanese surrender document signed on September 12, 1945 at Municipal Building.

CHAPTER FOURTEEN

Japanese Surrender

By early 1945, supplies of raw materials being transported from Japanese-occupied territories to Japan were being intercepted by the Allies. The superior American naval and air power in the Pacific was gaining ascendency over the Japanese forces. American submarines and aircraft began to prey on Japanese shipping routes. From the American-occupied Iwo Jima, a B-29 Superfortress could carry 10,000 pounds (4,540 kg) of bombs over 3,000 miles (4,800 km), and this meant the Japanese mainland was exposed to constant Allied bombing raids.

Above: Japanese soldiers taken as prisoners of war in Burma, their faces reflecting a sense of defeat.

On April 1, 1945, the Americans landed at Okinawa, closer still to the Japanese mainland. The Japanese put up a strong resistance with 100,000 men and 2,000 aircraft in suicidal *Kamikaze* attacks. There were heavy casualties on both sides. On May 8, 1945, victory in Europe was formally declared and the Japanese were left alone to fight the Allies. Soon after, they lost their foothold in Burma. In June, Japan surrendered Okinawa.

The shortage of food and materials in Japan had been acute since late 1944. The Japanese Army deputy chief of staff declared in early 1945 that the war could not be prolonged beyond the spring of 1946 as Japan would face desperate food shortages.

The Japanese Cabinet realised that the Japanese capacity to continue fighting the war was seriously limited. But military hardliners determined to fight to the last man prevented an early conclusion to the war. It was only after two atomic bombs were dropped on Hiroshima and Nagasaki in August 1945 that the Japanese responded to the Allied demand to surrender.

Left: After suffering heavy casualties, the Japanese finally lost battles in Burma in May 1945. The British were very close to victory in Malaya.

On August 15, 1945, Japan's Emperor Hirohito conceded unconditionally. On September 2, 1945, on board the battleship USS *Missouri*, Japanese delegates signed the surrender document. The Second World War had finally ended.

The effect of the Japanese Occupation on the people in Singapore had been enormous. Apart from the suffering they had endured, their view of the British, the defeated master, had undergone tremendous change. When the British returned to Singapore, which had been their dominion for over 120 years, they had to come to terms with a people whose thinking had gone beyond two empires.∎

Right: B-29s of the Allied Forces carried out raids on Singapore from late 1944. To the people, these bombings, uninterrupted by Japanese anti-aircraft fire, were signs that the tide of war was turning.

Below (left and right): Leaflets were dropped from the air to inform Japanese soldiers and Singapore residents that Germany had surrendered on May 7, 1945.

BOMBING BY THE B-29S

"I think it was about 1944, then came 1945, so we started to see these B-29s. They only dropped these incendiary bombs. We could watch from our office. Oh, it was quite a sight, looking at the incendiary bombs. They first drop as a big canister and then slowly it breaks off and drill sticks were scattered. And then the moment it touches some object, it will get alighted.

"The Japanese fighters try to intercept, also cannot reach them. We just watch to see how they try to shoot at the B-29s. Then, not long after, there was one plane came with leaflets, raining down from the sky telling that the Japanese have lost the war."

—*Chin Sin Chong, clerk*, Butai 15848

Left: On August 6, 1945, the Allies dropped an atomic bomb on Hiroshima and three days later on Nagasaki.

Below: As a result of the atomic bombs, the Japanese surrendered unconditionally on August 15, 1945 and the British counter-attack in Malaya did not take place. The Japanese laid down their arms and further bloodshed was avoided in Malaya and Singapore.

Opposite (top and bottom): On September 12, 1945, the Japanese delegation, led by General Seishiro Itagaki, formally surrendered to Admiral Lord Louis Mountbatten, Supreme Allied Commander in Southeast Asia, at the Municipal Building.

JAPANESE LOSING THE WAR

"It was only in 1945 that I felt something strange was happening. In May, we received the order from the military to evacuate women and children. But they didn't tell us where they would be sending them on grounds of secrecy. The order came very suddenly to assemble by noon. We were all shocked, but I said goodbye to my wife and daughter. Afterwards, I learnt that they boarded a hospital ship, *Hime Maru*, heading for Japan.

"As for the men, we remained in Singapore to fight alongside the military if the enemy attacked. So we underwent military training. When I heard about Japan's surrender, I cried. But deep in my heart, I knew I was going to live. Until the day before, I didn't even know if I would survive if the enemy attacked. Of course, there were lots of things to worry about – how the English and the locals were going to treat us. But it was no use to worry. I was thankful that I was alive."

—*Kichijiro Ohmori, manager*

*Left and above: It was an emotional day for all who
had lived through the Japanese Occupation – finally, a
release from the tension, fear and suffering of nearly
four years.*

Right: Japanese soldiers, after laying down arms, marched to prison camps in Jurong and Malaya.

REVENGE

"At that time our people vented their anger at the Japanese. I saw it once myself at Arab Street. I happened to go there to buy things. There was a group of six or seven Japanese soldiers passing by. Our Chinese people saw them and shouted, 'Japanese soldiers, beat them up! Beat them up, don't let them go!' So they surrounded them and gave them a good beating.

"During the Japanese rule, they beat us and ordered us to kneel down. So they [the Chinese] asked them [Japanese soldiers] to do the same. There was one soldier who refused to do so and they kicked him and beat him up. I saw him kneel down and beg the Chinese not to beat him up. He kneeled there and said '*tolong*' [have mercy] and '*tabek*' [salute] to the Chinese. It was quite pitiful to see him beaten up by our Chinese. However, they were so cruel to us then."

—*Tan Ah Sang, housewife*

Left: Japanese POWs were set to work as labourers, clearing the streets and working at places like the harbour and the Padang. The former British POWs were brought in to supervise the Japanese POWs.

Top: A victory parade was organised by various communities to celebrate the end of the Japanese Occupation.
Bottom: On December 1, 1945, the Malayan People's Anti-Japanese Army was disbanded, and the British held a ceremony to thank them for their contribution to the war effort.

Right: On January 6, 1946, a ceremony took place in front of Municipal Building to honour the war-time fighting forces.

Below: Fifteen leaders of Force 136 and MPAJA were awarded British campaign medals.

Below (left): Chin Peng of the MPAJA headquarters was awarded the Burma Star and 1939–45 Star by Admiral Lord Louis Mountbatten.

Below (right): On January 13, 1946, the British gave Lim Bo Seng, the leader of the Force 136 Chinese agents, a grand funeral in front of Municipal Building to commemorate his contribution to the anti-Japanese resistance.

Right: The War Crimes Commission was set up to investigate the atrocities committed by the Japanese military. Search teams were sent out to exhume the bodies of British POWs and civilians who had been killed and buried.

Far right: For some families with missing loved ones, the identification of personal belongings recovered from mass graves crushed lingering hopes.

WAR CRIMES TRIAL

"About three weeks after the Japanese surrender, the newspapers reported that those people who were ill-treated by the Japanese during the Japanese Occupation could report to the South East Asia Criminal Investigation Court.

"At that time, there was a big mirror outside the Capitol Theatre. The photographs of the *Kempeitai* who ill-treated the people were pasted on that mirror. I went there and I could recognise eight of them. At that time, the [British] military headquarters already knew about my case. I was interviewed and a statement was made. It was not just one case, they put all cases concerning the *Kempeitai* ill-treated people together.

"The trial lasted over one week. We have about four or five persons as witnesses for our case. Among them, my statement was most important. I was beaten up by them. I demonstrated in the court how we were beaten up, how we were tortured by them. I took off my shirt to show them my wounds. Eventually, two of them were sentenced to death, the remaining five or six were imprisoned. After being in the prison for three years, they were sent back to Tokyo."

—*Lan Khong Kon, victim of the* Kempeitai

Above: Japanese military men believed to be responsible for war atrocities were put on trial.
Right: As many as 135 Japanese convicted of war crimes in Malaya and Singapore were executed.

Right: Japanese soldiers who died in action, including those executed, were buried in the Japanese cemetery at Philips Avenue.

Below: Those who died defending the island against the Japanese were buried in the Kranji War Memorial.

EPITAPH

Memorial to the Civilian Victims of the Japanese Occupation

"THIS MEMORIAL MARKS AN UNPRECEDENTED TRAGEDY IN THE HISTORY OF SINGAPORE.

"The occupation of Singapore by the Japanese Army between the 15th day of February, 1942 and the 18th day of August, 1945 was a dark and tragic epoch.

"The people of Singapore were subjected to lashing, humiliation, enslavement and extortion. Under the pretext of "mass screening" (*Sook Ching*), the Japanese Army massacred tens of thousands of non-combatants in secrecy. God was ridiculed. Civilisation was buried and the dignity of mankind trampled. Everywhere tears flowed. Everywhere blood splattered. And everywhere terror reigned.

"In January 1962, some of the remains of the civilian victims were first unearthed. This led to the setting up of a committee by the Singapore Chinese Chamber of Commerce for conducting further investigation for exhumation as well as for the planning of the construction of a mass grave and a memorial for the remains. In July the same year, a permit for exhumation was obtained from the Authority. In March 1963, the Singapore Government allotted a four acre plot of land for the site of this Memorial Park. During the last four years more and more remains of these victims were exhumed. In the meantime, as a result of the widespread response received from the public and the encouragement from the government who contributed to the Memorial Building Fund on the basis of a dollar to a dollar from the public, this memorial is eventually completed.

"Now this memorial stands towering over the Equator, gazing at the ever changing scenes of Southeast Asia and the world at large.

"Now this memorial stands aloft at this hub of communication between the Eastern and the Western Hemispheres, beckoning friendly day and night to the passers-by of Southeast Asia and the world.

"No one knows the exact number of our compatriots of the different races massacred during the dark days of the Occupation. Although countless sets of bones are already buried under this podium, it is most probable that they might represent only a fraction of the civilian victims massacred, whose number might be five or ten times greater. No one can list all our multiracial compatriots who were killed in the massacre. They deserve to be posthumously honoured as loyal, brave, virtuous and righteous men who have sacrificed their lives long before the independence of Singapore and should thus be enshrined in the spiritual foundation of the country.

"The four towering columns of this memorial symbolise loyalty, bravery, virtue and righteousness, traits of which are reflected in the traditional harmony and solidarity of the multiracial, multi-cultural and multi-religious society of Singapore.

"This memorial stands to prove that the people of Singapore were able to hold their own together in adversity and it also signifies their ever-readiness to share the common prosperity of the country in future.

"Let this memorial echo the voice of the people of Singapore.

"War is evil. Peace is sacred. The big and the strong nations want to live, so do the small and weak ones. The big and strong ones who oppress the small and weak ones will never escape condemnation and punishment on the final judgement of history. However, the best policy is to redress grievances amicably and not to generate enmity. The people of Singapore are always with the peoples of the world, including the people of Japan, who are peace loving and who oppose aggression, imperialism and colonialism.

"May the souls of the civilian victims of the Japanese Occupation rest in eternal peace and accept this epitaph dedicated to them by the people of Singapore."

—Pan Shou (translated by C.M. Wong)

This was written in 1965 by Pan Shou on the request of Soon Peng Yam, then president of the Singapore Chinese Chamber of Commerce. The intention was to have it carved on the Cenotaph. However, this did not materialise. This text was eventually published in the Nanyang Journal *in 1984.*

Student representatives pay their respects at the foot of the Cenotaph at Beach Road on February 15, 1996.

Tears stained flower crimson like
    And blood tainted the blue ocean
Ye wandering souls who rise with the tide
    Shall guard this young emerging nation.

        —Pan Shou, written in 1965 (translated by C.M. Wong)

Select Bibliography

This is a select bibliography of materials available in the English language, with a few exceptions in Chinese or Japanese. More Chinese language texts are listed in the Chinese edition of this book.

ARCHIVAL MATERIALS FROM THE NATIONAL ARCHIVES

British Military Administration. *Chinese Affairs.* NA 868–NA 879.

British Military Administration Files. *Social Affairs Department.* MSA 001–026.

I.P.D. (Indian Passive Defence Service Corps) dissolution: presidential address, administration report, accounts. September 1942.

McNiece, Percy. *A Nip in the Air 1942–1945.* Memoirs, undated.

Nankwang Weekly Nos 1–117, 1942–1945.

Singapore Improvement Trust Files 1942–1945. KKK 10057–10375.

Syonan Jit Poh 1941–1945.

Syonan Sinbun 1942–1945.

Tessier, Francis. *An Unforgettable War Experience.* Memoirs, undated.

BOOKS

Barker, A.J. *Japanese Army Handbook 1939–1945.* London: Ian Allan Ltd, 1979.

Benda, Harry J. (editor). *Japan Military Administration in Indonesia: selected documents.* New Haven: Yale University Southeast Studies, 1965.

Cheah Boon Kheng. *Red Star Over Malaya: resistance and social conflict during and after the Japanese Occupation 1941–1946.* Singapore: Singapore University Press, 1983.

Chen Su Lan. Remember Pompong and Oxley Rise. Singapore: Chen Su Lan Trust, 1969.

Chop Suey. (Illustrated by Liu Kang.) 3 vols. Singapore: Printed at Ngai Seong Press, 1946. (A selection from a list of gruesome events that happened in Malaya during the Japanese Occupation.

Chua Ser Koon (editor). *Malayan Chinese resistance to Japan 1937–1945, selected source materials.* Singapore: Cultural & Historical Publishing House, 1984.

Construction of the Greater East Asia Co-prosperity Sphere. Tokyo: Mainichi Publishing Co., 1943.

Cruickshank, Charles. Special Operations Executives in the Far East. London: Oxford University Press, 1983.

Dean, H.R. *The Royal New Zealand Air Force in Southeast Asia 1941–42.* Wellington:

War History Branch, Department of Internal Affairs, 1952.

Good Citizens' Guide. Singapore: *Syonan Sinbun*, 1943.

Jones, F.C. *Japan's New Order in East Asia: Its Rise and Fall 1937–45*. London: Oxford University Press, 1954.

Kawamura Saburo. *Climbed the Thirteen Steps: Reminiscences of a War Criminal*. 1952. (Japanese text.)

Lee Geok Boi. *Syonan: Singapore Under the Japanese, 1942–1945*. Singapore: Landmark Books, 1992.

Robertson, Eric. *The Japanese File: Pre-war Japanese Penetration in Southeast Asia*. Hongkong: Heinemann Asia, 1979.

Shinozaki, Mamoru. *My Wartime Experience in Singapore*. (Oral history programme.) Singapore: Institute of Southeast Asian Studies, 1973.

Singapore Shiseikai Club (editor). *The History of Syonan Municipal Administration: Occupation of Singapore*. Tokyo: Japan Singapore Association, 1986. (Japanese text.)

Syonan: Singapore Under the Japanese. A Catalogue of Oral History Interviews. Singapore: Oral History Department, 1986.

Tan Thoon Lip. *Kempeitai "kindness"*. Singapore: *The Malayan Law Journal*, 1946.

Tan Yeok Seong. *The Extortion by Japanese Military Administration of 50,000,000 from the Chinese in Malaya*. Singapore: Nanyang Book Co. Ltd, 1947.

Trenowden, Ian. *Malayan Operations Most Secret – Force 136*. Singapore: Heinemann Asia, 1978.

Ward, Ian. *The Killer They Called A God*. Singapore: Media Masters, 1992.

Wilson, Harold. *Educational Policy and Performance in Singapore 1942–1945*. (ISEAS occasional paper no. 16.) Singapore: Institute of Southeast Asian Studies, 1973.

ARTICLES

Akashi, Yoji. Bureaucracy and the Japanese Military Administration, with specific reference to Malaya. *Japan in Asia 1942–1945*. Singapore: Singapore University Press, 1981, pp. 46–82.

Akashi, Yoji. Education and indoctrination policy in Malaya and Singapore under the Japanese rule. *Malaysian Journal of Education* 13 no. 1/2: 1–46, December 1976.

Akashi, Yoji. Japanese policy towards the Malayan Chinese, 1941–1945. *Journal of Southeast Asian Studies* 1 no. 2: 61–89, September 1970.

Lee Ting Hui. Singapore under the Japanese 1942–1945. *The Journal of South Seas Society* 17: 31–69, April 1961.

Leong, Stephen. The Malayan Overseas Chinese and the Sino-Japanese War 1937–1941. *Journal of Southeast Asian Studies* 10 no. 2: 293–320, 1979.

Wong Lin Ken. The Fall of Singapore: A Wider Historical Perspective. *Commentary* no. 3: 2–8, March 1979.

Acknowledgements

This publication would not have been possible without the contributions of the following people who were interviewed for the oral history project on the Japanese Occupation of Singapore:

Mitsuo Arai
Chan Cheng Yean
Mdm Chew Lee Ngor
Chia Chore Seng
Kenneth Chia Jai Nen
Chin Sin Chong
Robert Chong
Mrs Elizabeth Choy
Mdm Chu Shuen Choo
Herman Marie de Souza
Carl Francis de Souza
Cleaver Rowell Eber
Mdm Foo Hee Hong
Daniel Fraser
Gay Wan Guay
Patrick Hardie
Ismail Zain
Koh Soh Goh
Lan Khong Kon
Lee Chui Tong
Lee Han Kong
Lee Kip Lin
Liau Thai Chuan
Lim Chok Fui
Lim Hoon
Lim Ming Joon
Lim Seng
Lim Soo Gan
Neoh Teik Hong
Ng Aik Huan
Dr F.A.C. Oehlers
Kichijiro Ohmori
Alfred Devadasan Ponnambalam
Colonel P K Saghal
See Hong Peng
Soh Chuan Lum
Soon Kim Seng
Fujiwara Takashi (Nagase Takashi)
Tan Ah Sang
Tan Guan Chuan
Victor Tan

Tan Wah Meng
Teo Choon Hong
Teong Ah Chin
Stanley Warren

PICTURE CREDITS

The National Archives is grateful to the following people and institutions for the photographs and artifacts reproduced in this book. Illustrations not listed belong to the National Archives. [T,C,B (top, centre, bottom); L,R (left, right)]

Australian War Memorial: 53, 54 (T)
Broadhurst, Douglas: 170 (B)
Broome, Richard: 165
Chan Chon Hoe: 175 (B L & R)
Chan, Elizabeth: 25 (B L)
Chang Teh Cheok: 46 (B), 167 (B)
Chapman, Spencer: 170 (B)
Chelliah, S.: 4 (T), 83 (T), 85, 86, 87, 88 (T L & B R), 89 (C), 110 (B L & R), 114 (T), 116 (T R), 123 (T), 143 (B), 145 (T R & B), 162 (T)
Cheong Yew Kee: 2, 6–7, 36 (B), 40 (C), 49 (T & C)
Chew Ann Sim: 148 (T R & B)
Chin Kang Hui-kuan: 42 (T L)
Choy, Elizabeth: 55 (T)
Chu Chiu Lam: 71 (B R)
Chu Sui Mang: 100 (T R)
Chua Peng Liang: 71 (B L)
Chuang Hui Tsuan: 132 (T & C)
Cruickshank, Charles: 169 (B L & R)
Davis, John: 167 (T)
Ennis, Elizabeth: 65 (T)
Francoise, Sister: 104 (T R)
Gay Wan Guay: 137 (T L)
Gay Wan Leong: 121 (B L & R)
Goh Han Min: 82 (T R & B)
Haxworth, W.R.M.: 64 (B L & R), 65 (B L)
Heng Chiang Ki: 119 (B L)

Ho Kwai Mun: 16 (C)
Ibrahim Isa: 105 (B R), 150 (C L & R), 162 (B)
Images of Singapore Gallery, Sentosa: 172
Imperial War Museum: 22, 23, 24 (C L), 26, 27, 28, 29, 30, 31, 34, 36 (T), 37, 40 (B), 41, 42 (T R), 43 (T), 45 (B), 48 (T), 52 (B), 54 (C & B R), 56 (T & C R), 57, 58 (T & B L), 59 (C), 62 (T), 73, 76 (T), 77 (T L), 78, 79, 131, 154, 164, 169 (T R), 173, 174, 175 (T), 176 (T), 177, 178, 179, 180, 181, 182 (T, C & B L), 183 (B L & R)
Ishibe, Toshiro: 97, 98
Karuppiah, N.: 88 (T R & B L)
King, Herbert Lawrence: 25 (C)
Lee Hin Meng: 20
Lee Khee Yoon: 103 (C R), 158
Lee Pey Yuen: 142 (R), 143 (T)
Lee Siew Hong: 90 (B L), 152 (B L)
Lee Teck Seng: 148 (T L)
Lee, Steven: 187
Leong Leng: 105 (L), 129 (T & B R), 163 (B R)
Leong, William: 82 (T L)
Lim Leong Geok: 166, 168 (B L)
Lim Seng: 99 (B)
Lim Soo Gan: 25 (T), 90 (B R)
Liu Kang: 72 (T), 99 (T R), 100 (T L)
Loh Teck Cheong: 104 (B), 144, 145 (T L), 146 (T L & R), 152 (T L & R)
Mainichi Sinbun, Tokyo: 146 (B)
Mak Yit: 129 (B L)
Marcus, P.C.: 83 (B)
Nanyang Siang Pau: 89 (T), 147 (T), 148 (C), 150 (T)
Nathan, S.R.: 89 (B)
National Museum: 117 (T R)
National University of Singapore Department of Social Medicine and Public Health: 60 (T), 61
Ng Aik Huan: 16 (B R)
Ng Sin Yue & Soh Chuan Lam: 8, 106
Ng Yiok Hee: 151 (T)

Oehlers, F.A.C.: 138 (B), 139 (T)
Paglar, Eric: 94
Parrish, Edward Ivor: 62 (B L & R), 65 (C R)
People's Association: 84, 176 (B)
Quah Wee Ho: 24 (B), 161 (T L), 171 (T L & R)
Seah Keok Ann, David: 4 (B), 18
Shinozaki, Mamoru: 138 (T R)
Si Ma Chun Ying: 71 (T)
Singapore Chinese Chamber of Commerce: 183 (T L & R)
Singapore Swiss Club: 56 (C L), 58 (B R)
Soh Chuan Lam: 116 (T L & badges at B L), 117 (T L), 118 (T R & B), 119 (T L & R)
Straits Times Library: 169 (T L)
Syed Hussein: 104 (T L)
Tan Keng Hoe: 90 (C L), 91 (T L)
Tan Kok Kheng: 12, 13 (B), 14 (T), 15
Tan Lai Huat: 113 (B R), 119 (B R)
Tan Peng Koon: 122 (T R)
Tan Teck Seng: 91 (T R & B), 105 (T R), 126 (T L), 130 (T R), 136 (B), 137 (T R), 163 (T R)
Tan Wee Eng: 150 (B)
Tan, Victor: 24 (T)
Tay Yen Hoon: 103 (T R & C L), 128
Teo Siew Jin: 55 (B)
Teong Ah Chin: 14 (B), 16 (T)
Tham Sien Yen: 168 (T)
Urquhart, M.Y.: 56 (B)
Vincent, Brother: 54 (B L), 65 (B R)
Warren, Stanley: 63, 64 (T)
Woo, Louise: 16 (B L)
Woon Wai Tao: 130 (T L)
Yeo Eng Choon: 142 (L), 162 (C L)
Yeo Guan Chin: 163 (T L & B L)
You Wai Kee: 13 (T)
Yu Yu Ching: 19 (T)

Index

191